Ambiti
Julius
Shaped the Ancient World, and Impacted the Modern One

By Jack Johnson

©Copyright 2016 WE CANT BE BEAT LLC

Copyright 2016 by Jack Johnson.

Published by WE CANT BE BEAT LLC

Krob817@yahoo.com

Table of Contents

Introduction 5

Chapter 1 13

The Early Life of Julius Caesar 13

Chapter 1 30

The Early Life of Julius Caesar 30

Chapter 3 47

Becoming A Politician 47

The First Triumvate 65

Chapter 5 80

The Gallic Wars 80

Chapter 6 98

Caesar's Civil War 98

Chapter 7 115

Old Enemies and New Allies 115

Chapter 8 137

The Final Sweep 137

Chapter 9 155

Julius Caesar the Dictator	155
Chapter 10	174
The Aftermath of Assassination	174
Chapter 11	200
Modern Caesar	200
Bibliography	207

Introduction

You would think that someone who lived and died thousands of years ago couldn't remain relevant today. You would think the political and military strategies of civilizations that existed in a time before time couldn't possibly have such an influence on the strategies of our modern time. You couldn't possibly expect the name of someone whose life ended in a time where we put BC after the years, to be as relevant in today's world as it was when he was alive. You wouldn't expect Julius Caesar.

Julius Caesar is a name that everyone knows, and those who know who he was recognize what he did for civilization as it underwent dramatic change. Caesar defined one of the most significant periods of political revolution that ancient history knows. It is a time that acted as a testing ground for systems we still use today, no matter how altered. The Greeks operated on their democracy, everyone having an equal say in policy, while the Romans took a direction that more heavily mirrors what we see in many modernized countries today. One of the most tumultuous and fascinating periods of Roman history was the Roman Republic. This network of Senators represented their populations, or plebeians as the common middle class individual was referred to in these times, and worked as a political cabinet of policy makers. These elected officials were meant to converse, compromise, and govern in a way that represented the needs and the wants of the people. Caesar saw the potential of power within this system, and he took hold of it through brilliant political strategizing.

The truly breathtaking thing about Caesar's political influence is what was marked by his death. Caesar may have played with and manipulated the Roman Republic system to serve his needs, yet in death the system crumbled upon itself, and the Roman Empire was born from the ashes. It seems irrational and contested that one man could have such power over the political system that he literally changed the face of Roman politics forever, but Caesar makes the irrational possible.

Caesar's influence could have stopped at politics, and he would likely still be revered and studied just as much as he is today, but politics is not where it ended. The military prowess and his extensive military career is enough for multiple lifetimes, and it earned him the reputation of one of history's greatest military strategists. His conquests seemed impossible, yet he emerged victorious from the most dire of circumstances. What he did across what is now modern day Europe reshaped the lands politically, socially, and even geographically. These military quests shaped history and set the stage for decades of change after his death.

From humbling beginnings, Caesar was born into a family of no particular interest. The Caesar name knew little glory before Gaius Julius Caesar took it and made it the most recognizable name in the world for his time. When he was 16 Caesar's father died suddenly, and his political career was forced to take a jumpstart. In the middle of his adolescence Caesar was already learning how to play the political game.

His early life also saw military combat, heroic bravery, and even capture by pirates. He was awarded a small taste of power before even getting out of his teenage years, and this power he wouldn't forget as it would continue to drive him and his exploits.

Caesar's political rise was relatively quick. He quickly saw the weaknesses in the senatorial structure, and knew just what to do to take advantage of it. Bribery and deceit were already fairly commonplace amongst the Roman Senate, but Caesar orchestrated more cunning versions of the two vices than any of his predecessors. Through one of history's most ingenious political alliances Caesar instigated unprecedented change within Roman politics. His tactics were unsavory to say the least, and it put him under the scrutiny of his colleagues. Before they could do anything about him, though, Caesar was off to begin the next, and possibly greatest, chapter of his life.

After his abuse of the Republican system, Caesar set out to conquer the Eastern territories of Gaul in his famed Gallic Wars campaign. Caesar's actions would secure his role as the world's most powerful conqueror, but it would also shake up his political stability as his alliances began to crash. The Roman Senate finally had enough and demanded that Caesar relinquish his armies and return to Rome to be tried for his political actions before the campaign. Caesar refused, and with the crossing of the Rubicon River started his own civil war against Rome.

This Civil War would rage for years with Caesar never once coming close to seceding victory. He took hold of the capitol, and then set out after his enemies. His campaign eventually brought him to

Egypt where Cleopatra changed his life forever. Caesar and the Egyptian queen Cleopatra fell into one of history's most fiery love affairs, and it spurred Caesar to wage war in Egypt against those who wanted to oust Cleopatra and give total power to her brother, Ptolemy.

Caesar claimed his victory over the Egyptians, adding another army to crumble beneath his weight. His escapades were not over, and he set off even further East to continue stomping out the enemies which he had scattered in the civil war. After a few more decisive victories Caesar brought his civil war to a close, and returned to Rome to begin his reign as dictator. Caesar completely took control of Roman politics, and disregarded the Senate left and right to unapologetically push through his own agenda. He felt unstoppable and untouchable, but only months after his return to the capitol, he would find neither of these things to be true.

On March 15th, 44 BC, Caesar was stabbed 23 times by a group of Senators who had conspired to end his rule, and his life. Caesar's death shook the Roman world at its foundation, and the state crumbled into disarray with multiple parties contending for the incredible power left in his wake that was now up for grabs. Octavian, Caesar's distant nephew and heir to his fortune, managed to secure victory in this power struggle, and his rule saw the final collapse of the Roman Republic. The death of Julius Caesar and the subsequent rule by his heir gave birth to the Roman Empire.

Caesar lived a truly incredible and seemingly impossible life. He had lifetime's worth of accomplishments, and had such a dramatically sweeping influence on the world, that it's no wonder we are tantalized and endlessly fascinated with his story. His life encompasses all the workings of a thrilling tale of political espionage, a harrowing escapade of military conquest and action, and even melodramatic romances. His life, in all of its ways, was perplexing, exciting, and proof that reality can be far more unbelievable than fiction.

Chapter 1

The Early Life of Julius Caesar

It may seem odd that a man whose life had such influence and prowess didn't come from particularly luxurious beginnings. Then again, it might not seem odd. Maybe it takes a simple and quiet early life to mold a man nearly capable of conquering the world, as was the case with Gaius Julius Caesar, born on July 12th, 100 BC into the family of the Julii Caesares. This family lineage, while of patrician status, meaning they were part of the wealthier elite as opposed to the lower class plebeians, or plebes, had no great influence on the politics of their time. What little influence they had only stemmed from three consulships.

In the Roman Republic, a consul was a member of office who was considered the highest ranking. At the time it was the highest elected political office a man could earn. Consul's elections were held every year in which two consuls would be elected to serve alongside one another for a one year term. Considering the rapid turnover of this political position, it is not exactly a feat that the Caesares' had only had three.

Caesar didn't grow up with particularly heavy political influence in his life. It played its role in his adolescence, but he would by and large see the most success compared to anyone who bared the name before him. His own parents had their political ties, but nothing astounding. His father, who was also named Gaius Julius Caesar, was able to achieve the ranking of praetor in his lifetime. This was the second highest ranking of all the Roman Republic's elected magistrates. Praetors were elected officials who were given all sorts of duties both domestically and abroad. Caesar's father, in particular, enacted his governance on the province of Asia.

Caesar's father certainly was a role model in Caesar's life, but his more by the book tactics would quickly be left in the dust by his son's riskier and more progressive strategies. In terms of his stately character and renowned charisma, Julius Caesar almost certainly got that from his mother, Aurelia Cotta. While not a particularly influential member of the political system herself, Aurelia came from a family that had a history of sway on Roman politics, producing a number of consuls and other political officials. Both Aurelia's grandfather and father had served as consuls at a time, and a number of her half-brothers had done the same.

Truly, it is Aurelia who raised the young Julius Caesar. Caesar's father was often gone, away on state business in a time when travel was slow and communication was slower. Very little is known about the early childhood of Caesar, but we can be certain that it was Aurelia and her family who cared for Caesar and instilled him with the charm, character, and incredibly unique tactfulness that made him who he was.

.   .   .

While Caesar's bloodline might not have run too thick in the political landscape, his cultural heritage was and is something to write home about. The gens Julia family proclaimed themselves to be descendants of Iulus, a prominent figure in Roman mythology. Iulus was the son Aeneas, who stakes his place in history as a renowned Trojan hero. Aeneas appears all throughout Greek and Roman mythology. Virgil's *Aeneid* tells us that Aeneas was one of the only Trojans who was not killed or captured when the city of Troy was overtaken and destroyed. He then went on to form the Aeneads, a powerful army with a long history in the politics and war mongering of the mythology. He also appears in Homer's *The Iliad,* but only as a minor character. Regardless, he and his bloodline comprise a major part of a culture held dear and true to the hearts of the Roman people. For the Caesar's to claim descension from this lineage is a mighty claim that likely had to do with the patrician status they held throughout their existence.

Even the name Julius Caesar holds meaning behind it that enriches the cultural heritage of Caesar's family. It can be interpreted to refer to three different attributes of the first Caesar. One interpretation is that the first Caesar wore a dense head of hair atop his head. Caesaries is Latin for hair. Another says that our original Caesar had incredibly distinguishable eyes which glowed a radiant grey. This piercing gaze could have earned him the name given that the Latin translation for eyes is oculis caesiis. The last interpretation is the one that Julius Caesar likely preferred the most. Ancient literature suggests that this man who first bore the name Caesar earned the name after slaying an elephant in the midst of battle. Elephant in Moorish translates to caesari. Given the elephant imagery that persisted throughout Caesar's aesthetic taste, it is likely that this interpretation is what struck him as the most unique and probably the most enticing for Caesar's battle ready mind.

It is likely that the Caesar name wasn't one that was thrown around a whole lot in this time. Patrician families all across the Roman Republic knew wealth, fame, and power much greater than this family of low ranking origin that didn't do much more than simply come from wealth. That was, until Julius Caesar. No event that occurred in the year 100 BC would be more influential in the grand scheme of things than the birth of this man.

. . .

Caesar wasn't born during the most politically stable of times in the Roman Republic, and this may have unwittingly set the stage for him to have such a rapid rise to success. Conflict was raging and amassing at both fronts of Roman territory, as well as domestically, creating a firestorm of political turmoil. On the Western front there was a conflict being fought named the Social War. This war persisted from 91 BC to 88 BC, and it saw the forces of the Roman Republic engaging in vicious battle with various Italian cities. There had been long standing friction between the Romans and many of the Italian cities they conquered in the Samnite Wars, a series of engagements that gave Rome its domineering power over the Italian peninsula. These cities had been given their independence, yet were still expected to aid Rome with any resources or expenses they requested. This eventually blew up and led to three years of conflict that would only be the start of a period of immense tension.

To the East, King Mithridates of Pontus was rifling feathers in Bithynia with plots to overthrow Nicomedes IV, a rule who had only been put in power by the Romans to be bent to their will. Busy fighting the Social War, Rome had to depend on its forces in their Asian provinces to fight these battles. Mithridates certainly put up a fight, and his actions and timing would have grave effects on the Republic.

None of this conflict was helped, in fact it was made a whole lot worse by and because of, what is perhaps the worst of these clashes going on at the time. The Roman Republic was staunchly divided in its politics at this juncture in time. Two factions of politicians dominated the era, and they were the optimates and the populares. The ideals of these two parties couldn't have been further from each other. The optimates were a party built on conservative principles. Their main interest was in the wealthy elite, and much if not all of their policy held their interests in mind above any others. It was a party built on control and a rigid authority. Optimates saw the Senate as a tool for commanding great power over a growing number of people. Some probably even saw it as a weapon for doing so.

Meanwhile, the populares existed at the opposite end of this spectrum. They were a progressive party that would, by today's standards, be considered much more "for the people." Rather than holding the interests of the upper class to any standard, the populares stood for the general population of the Republic. They were advocates of change, and constantly strived for political, economic, and social reform when the system wasn't benefitting the majority of the population.

This political rift would cut like a knife through the Republic's foreign and domestic stability, and there were two men driving this knife ever deeper, and making that tear a whole lot wider. These men were Gaius Marius, a popularis, and Lucius Cornelias Sulla, an optimas and, ironically, the protégé of Marius. The Marius name had taken up a spot alongside the Caesar name after Marius married Julia Caesaris, Caesar's aunt. It may have seemed beneficial to have an extension of your family be as wealthy and as politically influential as Gaius Marius, a man who held consul a record seven times, yet he would eventually come to regret this tie.

Marius' claim to fame at the time of Caesar's adolescence was his decisive victories in the Social

War. His success here made him a viable candidate to lead the armies in the East who were preparing to do battle with Mithridates. The Senate was faced with the choice of either sending him or Sulla, the consul at the time who also had a decorated military history. They initially chose Sulla, but through some back-handed political maneuvering Marius was able to organize an assembly which appointed him instead. Furious at this injustice, Sulla ignored the assembly's decision and left for the city of Nola where a massive army lay in wait for a commanding general to lead them into battle against Mithridates. When Sulla arrived in Nola, though, he presented slightly different plans.

He convinced them to ignore the assembly's decree and fall in line behind him as he led them back to Rome. With a force of six legions backing him, Sulla wasn't coming home in a bid for peace. He had every intention of returning to commence a civil war, and that is just what he did. Marius was, unsurprisingly, caught off guard by this sudden force.

This was the first time in history that Roman soldiers had attacked their own city, and Marius was in no way prepared for such an unheard of and downright treasonous act. He attempted to amass an army, but to no avail as he was quickly driven out of the city in bloody conflict. Sulla marched into the city with fire in his eyes, going on a murderous rampage, spilling the blood of all those who defied him, and had defied him in the past. Sulla, through unprecedented force, reclaimed Rome for himself, and Marius barely escaped with his life.

     Satisfied with his accomplishments at home, it was time for Sulla to get to the matter at hand. Soon after reclaiming the city, he marched out of it to head East, back towards Mithridates. With the clock ticking on the Eastern front, as Mithridates forces grew stronger and stronger, Sulla neglected to establish much political stability before he left. The divide between the optimates and populares was still very prominent, and Sulla had only made it to Greece before fighting once again broke out back home. As the fighting continued unchecked Marius, who had been hiding out in Africa, amassing an army there, saw his chance to return to Rome. He made his grand return and with the help of the populares supporters, overthrew Sulla's supporters, going as graphically far as to put the party leader's heads on display in the Forum. Marius had completed a bloody campaign to take back Rome, and yet it would end up being his last great accomplishment. In 86 BC, seventeen days after being elected to his seventh consulship, Gaius Marius died.

It is profound to think that as all this transpired, all this bloodshed, all this turmoil and uncertainty, there was young Julius Caesar watching it all. To a child, the intricate geopolitical workings of this system probably made little sense, yet there is no doubt the landscape had an effect on little Caesar. To witness the first Roman civil war in history at that young of an age must have had a profound impact on the boy, and without witnessing these events he likely wouldn't have become the man that he was. From a young age Caesar was well aware of the influence of power, politics, and war.

It was in 85 BC, a year after Marius' death, that a much more significant death rocked Caesar's world and launched a dramatic new chapter in his life. One morning changed everything for Caesar forever. It was on this morning that, as he put on his shoes, Caesar's father abruptly and unexpectedly collapsed. There had been no apparent cause for what had just happened, but in an instant Caesar was fatherless. He was only sixteen years old when suddenly a huge financial and emotional weight was placed on his shoulders. Just like that he was the head of the family, and had no choice but to act quickly and begin to contribute in any way he could. In 84 BC he was elected the new High Priest of Jupiter, as the previous one had been killed during Marius' spree of vengeance on Sulla's supporters. Caesar was now part of this system, and had been thrust full force into its rules and customs.

Since boyhood, Caesar had been betrothed to a plebian girl named Cossutia. She was a member of an equestrian family that possessed enticing wealth, yet because of her plebian status Caesar was forced to break it off. High priests were required to be married to a patrician, and so Caesar instead married Cornelia, the daughter of one of Marius' populares allies who helped him reclaim the city. This position wasn't a flashy one and it didn't give Caesar much, if any, political influence, but it did allow him to put bread on the table. He of course wanted to carry on his father's legacy, and this seemed like a good starting point. However, Caesar was forced to stand by and watch as more political turmoil occurred out of his control.

While Marius took back Rome, only to die shortly after, Sulla continued to do battle with Mithridates to the East. Sulla, a figure whose military prowess absolutely can't be denied, saw violent victory of Mithridates, and afterwards was prepared to return to Rome with one intent in mind. He was beset on finishing what he started, and ending this civil war with the ousting of the late Marius' supporters.

Sulla and his army, who already had one major victory under their belt, led a successful campaign across Italy, and in 82 BC he reclaimed Rome. Rather than returning to the old ways that had led to such violent back and forth conflict, Sulla took his powergrab one step further. He proclaimed himself dictator, a position that hadn't been known in Rome for quite some time. The role had been held in the Republic's history before, but for no longer than six month periods. Dictators were elected by the Senate in harrowing times that called for forceful rule. This often applied to things like rebellions and mutinies, and was by no means a common practice. It ended sometime after the Second Punic War, and took a circumstance as grave as the Roman Civil War to be reinstated. However, Sulla brought the tradition back with a twist. His appointment was indefinite.

Sulla brought down the proverbial hammer on Rome as he claimed complete and total power over the Republic. He made sure his reclamation matched the aggression and fury of Marius' years before by wiping Marius' presence and history from the city. He had all statues of the man destroyed, and his body was even tossed into the Tiber river. Sulla then began his own rampage set to wipe out all of his enemies, executing and exiling them through his unabashedly harsh proscriptions. Sulla was indiscriminate with his revenge, wanting to get rid of everyone who had any sort of ties to Marius and his supporters. This of course included Caesar, the nephew of Marius and son-in-law to one of Marius' most prominent allies. Caesar saw the only accomplishments of his life stripped away from him as he lost his wife's dowry as well as his priesthood. Caesar wasn't going to stand for this however. He was ordered to divorce Cornelia, but resisted, and instead was exiled from Rome. Caesar was only a teenager and already he had a price on his head.

Thankfully, this didn't last long. With the help of his mother's influence, the threats against Caesar were abolished. Sulla was highly reluctant, but he pardoned Caesar and lifted all ill wishes against him. Caesar was in a position to start his political career anew, now that he was supposedly free of harm. But Caesar wasn't a fool, and he wasn't going to take his chances in a city where he had seen so much violence and bloodshed, especially while the man in power was responsible for most of it. Caesar decided to leave behind his life in the city, and start on an entirely new endeavor. He left the patrician lifestyle to join the military.

Chapter 1

The Early Life of Julius Caesar

It may seem odd that a man whose life had such influence and prowess didn't come from particularly luxurious beginnings. Then again, it might not seem odd. Maybe it takes a simple and quiet early life to mold a man nearly capable of conquering the world, as was the case with Gaius Julius Caesar, born on July 12th, 100 BC into the family of the Julii Caesares. This family lineage, while of patrician status, meaning they were part of the wealthier elite as opposed to the lower class plebeians, or plebes, had no great influence on the politics of their time. What little influence they had only stemmed from three consulships.

In the Roman Republic, a consul was a member of office who was considered the highest ranking. At the time it was the highest elected political office a man could earn. Consul's elections were held every year in which two consuls would be elected to serve alongside one another for a one year term. Considering the rapid turnover of this political position, it is not exactly a feat that the Caesares' had only had three.

Caesar didn't grow up with particularly heavy political influence in his life. It played its role in his adolescence, but he would by and large see the most success compared to anyone who bared the name before him. His own parents had their political ties, but nothing astounding. His father, who was also named Gaius Julius Caesar, was able to achieve the ranking of praetor in his lifetime. This was the second highest ranking of all the Roman Republic's elected magistrates. Praetors were elected officials who were given all sorts of duties both domestically and abroad. Caesar's father, in particular, enacted his governance on the province of Asia.

Caesar's father certainly was a role model in Caesar's life, but his more by the book tactics would quickly be left in the dust by his son's riskier and more progressive strategies. In terms of his stately character and renowned charisma, Julius Caesar almost certainly got that from his mother, Aurelia Cotta. While not a particularly influential member of the political system herself, Aurelia came from a family that had a history of sway on Roman politics, producing a number of consuls and other political officials. Both Aurelia's grandfather and father had served as consuls at a time, and a number of her half-brothers had done the same.

Truly, it is Aurelia who raised the young Julius Caesar. Caesar's father was often gone, away on state business in a time when travel was slow and communication was slower. Very little is known about the early childhood of Caesar, but we can be certain that it was Aurelia and her family who cared for Caesar and instilled him with the charm, character, and incredibly unique tactfulness that made him who he was.

. . .

While Caesar's bloodline might not have run too thick in the political landscape, his cultural heritage was and is something to write home about. The gens Julia family proclaimed themselves to be descendants of Iulus, a prominent figure in Roman mythology. Iulus was the son Aeneas, who stakes his place in history as a renowned Trojan hero. Aeneas appears all throughout Greek and Roman mythology. Virgil's *Aeneid* tells us that Aeneas was one of the only Trojans who was not killed or captured when the city of Troy was overtaken and destroyed. He then went on to form the Aeneads, a powerful army with a long history in the politics and war mongering of the mythology. He also appears in Homer's *The Iliad,* but only as a minor character. Regardless, he and his bloodline comprise a major part of a culture held dear and true to the hearts of the Roman people. For the Caesar's to claim descension from this lineage is a mighty claim that likely had to do with the patrician status they held throughout their existence.

Even the name Julius Caesar holds meaning behind it that enriches the cultural heritage of Caesar's family. It can be interpreted to refer to three different attributes of the first Caesar. One interpretation is that the first Caesar wore a dense head of hair atop his head. Caesaries is Latin for hair. Another says that our original Caesar had incredibly distinguishable eyes which glowed a radiant grey. This piercing gaze could have earned him the name given that the Latin translation for eyes is oculis caesiis. The last interpretation is the one that Julius Caesar likely preferred the most. Ancient literature suggests that this man who first bore the name Caesar earned the name after slaying an elephant in the midst of battle. Elephant in Moorish translates to caesari. Given the elephant imagery that persisted throughout Caesar's aesthetic taste, it is likely that this interpretation is what struck him as the most unique and probably the most enticing for Caesar's battle ready mind.

It is likely that the Caesar name wasn't one that was thrown around a whole lot in this time. Patrician families all across the Roman Republic knew wealth, fame, and power much greater than this family of low ranking origin that didn't do much more than simply come from wealth. That was, until Julius Caesar. No event that occurred in the year 100 BC would be more influential in the grand scheme of things than the birth of this man.

. . .

Caesar wasn't born during the most politically stable of times in the Roman Republic, and this may have unwittingly set the stage for him to have such a rapid rise to success. Conflict was raging and amassing at both fronts of Roman territory, as well as domestically, creating a firestorm of political turmoil. On the Western front there was a conflict being fought named the Social War. This war persisted from 91 BC to 88 BC, and it saw the forces of the Roman Republic engaging in vicious battle with various Italian cities. There had been long standing friction between the Romans and many of the Italian cities they conquered in the Samnite Wars, a series of engagements that gave Rome its domineering power over the Italian peninsula. These cities had been given their independence, yet were still expected to aid Rome with any resources or expenses they requested. This eventually blew up and led to three years of conflict that would only be the start of a period of immense tension.

To the East, King Mithridates of Pontus was rifling feathers in Bithynia with plots to overthrow Nicomedes IV, a rule who had only been put in power by the Romans to be bent to their will. Busy fighting the Social War, Rome had to depend on its forces in their Asian provinces to fight these battles. Mithridates certainly put up a fight, and his actions and timing would have grave effects on the Republic.

None of this conflict was helped, in fact it was made a whole lot worse by and because of, what is perhaps the worst of these clashes going on at the time. The Roman Republic was staunchly divided in its politics at this juncture in time. Two factions of politicians dominated the era, and they were the optimates and the populares. The ideals of these two parties couldn't have been further from each other. The optimates were a party built on conservative principles. Their main interest was in the wealthy elite, and much if not all of their policy held their interests in mind above any others. It was a party built on control and a rigid authority. Optimates saw the Senate as a tool for commanding great power over a growing number of people. Some probably even saw it as a weapon for doing so.

Meanwhile, the populares existed at the opposite end of this spectrum. They were a progressive party that would, by today's standards, be considered much more "for the people." Rather than holding the interests of the upper class to any standard, the populares stood for the general population of the Republic. They were advocates of change, and constantly strived for political, economic, and social reform when the system wasn't benefitting the majority of the population.

This political rift would cut like a knife through the Republic's foreign and domestic stability, and there were two men driving this knife ever deeper, and making that tear a whole lot wider. These men were Gaius Marius, a popularis, and Lucius Cornelias Sulla, an optimas and, ironically, the protégé of Marius. The Marius name had taken up a spot alongside the Caesar name after Marius married Julia Caesaris, Caesar's aunt. It may have seemed beneficial to have an extension of your family be as wealthy and as politically influential as Gaius Marius, a man who held consul a record seven times, yet he would eventually come to regret this tie.

Marius' claim to fame at the time of Caesar's adolescence was his decisive victories in the Social

War. His success here made him a viable candidate to lead the armies in the East who were preparing to do battle with Mithridates. The Senate was faced with the choice of either sending him or Sulla, the consul at the time who also had a decorated military history. They initially chose Sulla, but through some back-handed political maneuvering Marius was able to organize an assembly which appointed him instead. Furious at this injustice, Sulla ignored the assembly's decision and left for the city of Nola where a massive army lay in wait for a commanding general to lead them into battle against Mithridates. When Sulla arrived in Nola, though, he presented slightly different plans.

    He convinced them to ignore the assembly's decree and fall in line behind him as he led them back to Rome. With a force of six legions backing him, Sulla wasn't coming home in a bid for peace. He had every intention of returning to commence a civil war, and that is just what he did. Marius was, unsurprisingly, caught off guard by this sudden force.

This was the first time in history that Roman soldiers had attacked their own city, and Marius was in no way prepared for such an unheard of and downright treasonous act. He attempted to amass an army, but to no avail as he was quickly driven out of the city in bloody conflict. Sulla marched into the city with fire in his eyes, going on a murderous rampage, spilling the blood of all those who defied him, and had defied him in the past. Sulla, through unprecedented force, reclaimed Rome for himself, and Marius barely escaped with his life.

Satisfied with his accomplishments at home, it was time for Sulla to get to the matter at hand. Soon after reclaiming the city, he marched out of it to head East, back towards Mithridates. With the clock ticking on the Eastern front, as Mithridates forces grew stronger and stronger, Sulla neglected to establish much political stability before he left. The divide between the optimates and populares was still very prominent, and Sulla had only made it to Greece before fighting once again broke out back home. As the fighting continued unchecked Marius, who had been hiding out in Africa, amassing an army there, saw his chance to return to Rome. He made his grand return and with the help of the populares supporters, overthrew Sulla's supporters, going as graphically far as to put the party leader's heads on display in the Forum. Marius had completed a bloody campaign to take back Rome, and yet it would end up being his last great accomplishment. In 86 BC, seventeen days after being elected to his seventh consulship, Gaius Marius died.

    It is profound to think that as all this transpired, all this bloodshed, all this turmoil and uncertainty, there was young Julius Caesar watching it all. To a child, the intricate geopolitical workings of this system probably made little sense, yet there is no doubt the landscape had an effect on little Caesar. To witness the first Roman civil war in history at that young of an age must have had a profound impact on the boy, and without witnessing these events he likely wouldn't have become the man that he was. From a young age Caesar was well aware of the influence of power, politics, and war.

It was in 85 BC, a year after Marius' death, that a much more significant death rocked Caesar's world and launched a dramatic new chapter in his life. One morning changed everything for Caesar forever. It was on this morning that, as he put on his shoes, Caesar's father abruptly and unexpectedly collapsed. There had been no apparent cause for what had just happened, but in an instant Caesar was fatherless. He was only sixteen years old when suddenly a huge financial and emotional weight was placed on his shoulders. Just like that he was the head of the family, and had no choice but to act quickly and begin to contribute in any way he could. In 84 BC he was elected the new High Priest of Jupiter, as the previous one had been killed during Marius' spree of vengeance on Sulla's supporters. Caesar was now part of this system, and had been thrust full force into its rules and customs.

Since boyhood, Caesar had been betrothed to a plebian girl named Cossutia. She was a member of an equestrian family that possessed enticing wealth, yet because of her plebian status Caesar was forced to break it off. High priests were required to be married to a patrician, and so Caesar instead married Cornelia, the daughter of one of Marius' populares allies who helped him reclaim the city. This position wasn't a flashy one and it didn't give Caesar much, if any, political influence, but it did allow him to put bread on the table. He of course wanted to carry on his father's legacy, and this seemed like a good starting point. However, Caesar was forced to stand by and watch as more political turmoil occurred out of his control.

While Marius took back Rome, only to die shortly after, Sulla continued to do battle with Mithridates to the East. Sulla, a figure whose military prowess absolutely can't be denied, saw violent victory of Mithridates, and afterwards was prepared to return to Rome with one intent in mind. He was beset on finishing what he started, and ending this civil war with the ousting of the late Marius' supporters.

Sulla and his army, who already had one major victory under their belt, led a successful campaign across Italy, and in 82 BC he reclaimed Rome. Rather than returning to the old ways that had led to such violent back and forth conflict, Sulla took his powergrab one step further. He proclaimed himself dictator, a position that hadn't been known in Rome for quite some time. The role had been held in the Republic's history before, but for no longer than six month periods. Dictators were elected by the Senate in harrowing times that called for forceful rule. This often applied to things like rebellions and mutinies, and was by no means a common practice. It ended sometime after the Second Punic War, and took a circumstance as grave as the Roman Civil War to be reinstated. However, Sulla brought the tradition back with a twist. His appointment was indefinite.

Sulla brought down the proverbial hammer on Rome as he claimed complete and total power over the Republic. He made sure his reclamation matched the aggression and fury of Marius' years before by wiping Marius' presence and history from the city. He had all statues of the man destroyed, and his body was even tossed into the Tiber river. Sulla then began his own rampage set to wipe out all of his enemies, executing and exiling them through his unabashedly harsh proscriptions. Sulla was indiscriminate with his revenge, wanting to get rid of everyone who had any sort of ties to Marius and his supporters. This of course included Caesar, the nephew of Marius and son-in-law to one of Marius' most prominent allies. Caesar saw the only accomplishments of his life stripped away from him as he lost his wife's dowry as well as his priesthood. Caesar wasn't going to stand for this however. He was ordered to divorce Cornelia, but resisted, and instead was exiled from Rome. Caesar was only a teenager and already he had a price on his head.

Thankfully, this didn't last long. With the help of his mother's influence, the threats against Caesar were abolished. Sulla was highly reluctant, but he pardoned Caesar and lifted all ill wishes against him. Caesar was in a position to start his political career anew, now that he was supposedly free of harm. But Caesar wasn't a fool, and he wasn't going to take his chances in a city where he had seen so much violence and bloodshed, especially while the man in power was responsible for most of it. Caesar decided to leave behind his life in the city, and start on an entirely new endeavor. He left the patrician lifestyle to join the military.

Chapter 3

Becoming A Politician

Caesar's return to Rome saw his first step up the political staircase that was Roman politics. He was elected to the position of military tribune, a coveted position that was put in charge of militaristic representation and duties. All the tribunes had significant sway on politics, as they existed to balance the senate, checking them on their authority through a variety of facets, the most important being military matters. No position was more appropriate for Caesar to hold at the time, as he clearly knew what he was doing when it came to commanding an army and strategizing for war. He had also made it evident that he was a fast learner.

Caesar held this position for three years, before being elected as quaestor, moving up another rung of the ladder. This was a bit of a job switch for

Caesar, but necessary if he was to equip himself with the knowledge of all of Rome's political workings. The quaestor's duties were mostly financial, performing audits and organizing any and all financial affairs happening in the state. Quaestor would end up being a very fitting role for Caesar, and it likely is what sparked his interest in coinage. Many years later he would imprint his own image on Roman currency, as being that finely connected with the monetary system makes your power seem that much more far reaching.

Caesar's quaestorship was to be in the province of Hispania, serving under the rule of Antistius Vetus. Today we know this province as Spain. Caesar once again departed from the city that continued to call him home to pursue duties in another far off land. A great dissatisfaction set in for Caesar as his ship sailed into the Hispanian port. Caesar put forth his efforts as a quaestor for two years before his desire to be doing something more took over.

This was likely instigated by a statue of Alexander the Great that Caesar encountered while living in Hispania. Caesar felt a strong connection to this anciently revered figure, and had seen them as having very similar goals of conquest. What pained Caesar though was the fact that by the time Alexander was his age, he had conquered more than a young Caesar had even dreamed of. Caesar felt that, in comparison, he had hardly done anything with his life. He knew that if he was going to have statues of himself one day adorning the halls of the Forum, he had to aspire to be more than a quaestor. In Caesar's mind, time was slipping away, and he longed for the grand victories and unprecedented recognition that those like Alexander the Great enjoyed in their time.

This epiphany spurred Caesar to immediately request to be discharged from his duties before they were completed, and his request was granted. Political prestige was calling Caesar's name as he left

Hispania to return to Rome where he would jump full force back into politics.

. . .

It was an emotionally turbulent time for Caesar before he left for Hispania. Two deaths happened unfortunately close to one another, and certainly took their toll on Caesar. The first was his aunt Julia. An incredibly tasteful funeral was arranged for her, and it even displayed images of her late husband, Gaius Marius, images that had not been seen in the Republic ever since Sulla had all of Marius' likenesses removed.

At the funeral Caesar gave a powerful oration which paid due respect to his late aunt. This oration served another purpose too, however. In another show of bold confidence, Caesar used his speech to take jabs at Roman politicians, comparing and satirizing the idea of gods and kings and their comparable power.

"The family of my aunt Julia is descended by her mother from the kings, and on her father's side is akin to the immortal Gods; for the Marcii Reges [her mother's family name] go back to Ancus Marcius, and the Julii, the family of which ours is a branch, to Venus. Our stock therefore has at once the sanctity of kings, whose power is supreme among mortal men, and the claim to reverence which attaches to the Gods, who hold sway over kings themselves." This is how Caesar opened his speech, and just in this one snippet Caesar lets on his ideas of where power truly lies. Ultimate power and influence over populations came not just from political capacity, but religious authority as well. Caesar was working towards the power of a king, but what he wanted was the power of a God.

The second death occurred in the midst of Caesar's quaestorship, and it was one that hit Caesar even closer to his heart. His own wife, Cornelia, died giving birth to their second child in 69 BC. The child did not survive, and Caesar was left as the five year old Julia Caesaris' only parent. Julia would be raised by Aurelia, Caesar's mother.

. . .

In 67 BC Caesar was once again under the Roman sun. His next moves would be yet another demonstration of Caesar's incredible tactfulness and incredibly expansive knowledge of social and political systems. Caesar had never been particularly friendly with the majority of his political counterparts. The air of the Senate was still thick with tension between Caesar and the Sulla influenced majority who retained power over the Senate. His reputation with his political colleagues was not of great interest to Caesar, save for the few allies he needed to make sure he could set his plans into motion. Caesar knew that he didn't need the trust of those who sat around him in the Forum. He needed the trust of the people. Thus, this return to Rome was defined by Caesar's humanism and his public outreach.

In 66 BC Caesar became curator of the Appian Way. This was one of Rome's most strategically vital roads, as it marked the relatively safe passage from Rome to Brindisi. Roads were one of Roman civilization's greatest influences upon our modern world, and at the time they showed signs of true sophistication and civility. Caesar made sure the road was always maintained and made for convenient and worry free travel between the two cities. What better way to show voters arriving to Rome what you are doing for their well-being than have them come in on a road you strived to make as presentable as it is?

This extensive reconstruction obviously came at a price, and the hefty loan Caesar took out to improve the road began a series of debts that he would owe. No debts, political or financial, mattered to Caesar at a time when his only goal was building his image amongst the populace. He eventually earned the best position he could hold that enabled him to do this image forming. In 65 BC Caesar was elected aedile. Aedile's were the Roman officials who handled all maintenance of public buildings. The title also meant you were in charge of regulating all public events.

Caesar was an Aedile that did everything the people wanted, all at the expense of what the Senate wanted. Caesar spent lavishly on festivals and events to show who we really cared about. This money was, of course, borrowed, and Caesar's debt counter continued to rise, to no concern of Caesar's. He was winning the love and support of the voters, and that's all that mattered.

. . .

While Caesar built his public image, he also used the opportunities awarded to him to wash away as many remnants of Sulla as he could, doing everything in his relatively limited power at the time to return Marius' influence to the public eye. His greatest post-humous jab at Sulla came from his next marriage. Caesar married Pompeia, one of Sulla's granddaughters. By adding himself to the Sulla lineage in such a subtly devious way, Caesar reaffirmed that he had no limits.

Caesar used his position as aedile towards his anti-Sulla agenda in scrupulous ways. One of his most bold acts was to reinstate the trophies which Marius had procured from his victories. Caesar couldn't help but be amused at the idea of a Sullan Senate being forced to look at trophies won by one of their role model's greatest enemies. He of course also felt it right that his uncle's mark on Roman history be recognized and not forgotten, and it was of no concern to him how the Senate felt about that.

Caesar even used his legal prowess to attack those still benefitting from Sulla's indecent practices of his time. When Sulla announced his proscriptions upon taking Rome back from Marius, he not only squashed those who opposed him, but he lifted those who didn't. Many men were still bringing in huge financial benefits from these proscriptions, and Caesar sought to put a stop to that. He prosecuted multitudes of men, putting an end to illegal practices hiding in the framework of the Senate's policies.

.   .   .

Caesar was slowly becoming an eloquent master of manipulation and maneuvering to achieve the things he wanted to achieve. Through empty promises and shaky alliances he procured so much from such relatively small positions of power. However, with all of this under the table strategy came a reputation. Caesar was known amongst his political colleagues as a sneak and someone who only had his own best interest in mind. This reputation brought about a lot of scrutiny from the other members of the Senate, and many of them just sat in wait for the opportunity to indict the man and call him foul.

In 63 BC Quintus Lutatius Catulus thought he saw that opportunity. Marcus Tullius Cicero, consul at the time, had uncovered a conspiracy led by Lucius Sergius Catilina to overthrow the senate and take command of the Republic. Catulus had accused

Caesar of having a hand in these conspiracies, and sought to prove it, even though he had little more than a hunch to back up his accusations.

It was during a debate about what to do with the conspirators where the Senate's passionate distrust of Caesar really shone. Caesar was attending the debate, as he had been elected to begin a term as praetor in the following year. At one point Caesar was passed a note. Marcus Porcius Cato saw this and immediately jumped at what he thought was an opportunity to uncover Caesar for the conniving conspirator he was. Cato furiously demanded that the note which Caesar had just been passed be read out loud. Caesar, without hesitation, handed the note over to Cato, whose face quickly went white when he realized he was reading a love letter sent to Caesar by Cato's own half-sister, Servilia. The Senate's desperation to catch Caesar amidst his schemes only helped validate Caesar, and only served his public image.

A year after this debacle of a debate saw what Caesar could do to his accusers. A full year after the conspiracy had taken place, a commission was established to investigate what had occurred. Caesar's name was once again thrown around and accusations of his involvement were lobbed his way. In one last bout of embarrassment, Caesar's name was cleared by Cicero's evidence, and the whole thing was put to rest. That is, not before an accuser and one member of the investigative commission were hauled away to prison for what were considered treasonous crimes.

.   .   .

63 BC could reasonably be named the year of accusations for Julius Caesar. But such is the nature of the beast when you run for an office as esteemed as what Caesar achieved that year. 63 BC was the year of Caesar's campaign for Pontifex Maximus. This position was the highest rank a member of the Roman religion could hold. It came with great

religious influence, and an esteemed level of respect from magistrates and lawmakers alike. The position began as a wholly religious one, but became politicized over time. It was a position Caesar could do quite a bit with, and it would associate him one step closer to that God-like figure he was building himself up to be.

Running for Pontifex Maximus also put one more chip on the shoulder of Sulla's supporters, as Quintus Caecilius Metellus Pius, the man who formerly held the position, had been appointed by Sulla during his reign. Caesar's opponents in the race were two prominent figures in the optimate party whose intentions were to keep Sulla's influence alive and well through the position.

By this point Caesar was well aware of the dirty politics that had to be played to gain any sort of elected office, and he took out huge debts from a frighteningly large amount of individuals. It was a harrowing time for Caesar as he willingly put all of his eggs in one basket, banking on a victory to get him out of the indebted grave he was digging himself. If he didn't win the election it would likely result in his exile, as he simply owed too much for his campaign not to pay off. Lucky for him, it did. That year Caesar was elected Pontifex Maximus, likely because the vote was split between the two optimate candidates. With this new title Caesar was lifted further in the public eye, and his god-like comparisons were reaffirmed.

The position also earned him residence at the domus publicus. This exquisite lodging was located in the Via Sacra, ancient Rome's "main street" essentially. The house was neighbored by some of Rome's most significant religious buildings. The domus publicus would be a site of major scandal for Caesar, and result in some significant marital changes. In 62 BC the "good goddess" festival, known at the time as the Bona Dea, was held at Caesar's new home. This was a festival permitted to only women and, obviously, Caesar's wife Pompeia was in attendance. Despite the festival's gender specific policy, one man did manage to find his way in. Publius Clodius Pulcher, dressed like a woman, snuck into the festival. His intention, allegedly, was to seduce Pompeia. This brash plan went exactly how you'd expect, and Clodius was caught and accused of sacrilege, a crime for which he went to court.

Clodius came from an incredibly prominent patrician family, and Caesar had to choose carefully how he would deal with this tenuous situation. In legal respects, Caesar took no action. He declined to testify against Clodius in court. His non-involvement resulted in Clodius' acquittal. This isn't to say that Caesar did nothing about the circumstances, however. That same year Caesar divorced Pompeia. He proclaimed that, "the wife of Caesar must be above suspicion." It didn't matter whether the accusations and the scandal held any weight, the mere association with such heinous acts repulsed Caesar. His stance was firm and his actions were clear. The divorce was final and Caesar wasn't looking back. In fact, he was only looking ahead.

Caesar's next venture saw him back in Hispania in 61 BC, after being appointed governor of Hispania Ulterior, where he saw more military victory. Two factions were trying to gain control over the peninsula, and Caesar fought to quiet them both. The Callaici inhabited the northwestern corner of the peninsula, while the Lusitanians procured power in the West. Caesar quelled any fight these factions had in them. These conquests earned Caesar the highly respectable moniker of imperator. Imperators were similar in nature to commanders, and was more so a title that garnered respect and admiration. It was a title that suited Caesar nicely, and helped to strike fear into the hearts of his enemies.

Caesar's governance of Hispania was a highly respectable term that saw great victory and reform. His true political prowess shone in this time, and he made sure to end this position on a high note. Caesar left Hispania a respected leader, and his victories did not go unrecognized when he returned to Rome in 60 BC. Upon his return the Senate gave him the official title of imperator. With this title came a triumph for Caesar. While it was a literal triumph for his military and political careers, the triumph in reference is a Roman triumph specifically. Roman triumphs were public celebrations of decorated military leaders, and were meant as a kind of ceremony to honor one's latest accomplishments.

In another bold move, Caesar declined this triumph. To accept it meant he must remain a soldier of Rome, and could not hold any sort of political campaign. He wasn't even allowed to enter the city until the ceremony was meant to take place. The choice was easy. For Caesar, a big grandiose party was a worthwhile sacrifice to run for the highest office of the Roman Republic. With this title Caesar's power could grow to lengths it had yet to reach. It was an opportunity to get one step closer to being a God. Thus, in 60 BC Caesar relinquished his military position and rejoined politics, in a race for consulship.

The First Triumvate

If you ask historians about some of the greatest political maneuvering and strategizing of all time, they are pretty likely to refer you to Rome in 59 BC, when Caesar employed all his political assets at the time, and utilized all of his scrupulous cunning to secure Rome's highest elected office; the consulship. Caesar was able to pull this achievement off in daring ingenuity in large part thanks to two men, whom he had a history with. These men were Gnaeus Pompeius Magnus, known as Pompey, and Marcus Licinius Crassus. These two politicians, with their own histories of debts and favors, would align with Caesar and formed a secretive political alliance, so elusive it was practically melodramatic in fashion. This alliance came to be known as The First Triumvirate.

Before the Triumvirate was formed, Pompey's reputation around the Republic came primarily from his military success. His father had been a military general, but died when Pompey was only twenty, leaving him his estate and his obligations. Pompey made the most out of the hand he was dealt, and became a renowned military general under the Sulla ruled Rome. Pompey's conquests were known to be violent and domineering, as Pompey had a reputation for discounting the political ramifications of his actions, and only sought the glorious reputation that came with military conquest. He rightly earned that reputation, though, after helping to expand Rome's territories, and to defend against its enemies on multiple occasions.

One of Pompey's greatest achievements was his victory against King Mithridates VI in the Third Mithridatic War. He was nominated to take command over this conquest by the Senate, and largely supported by Caesar. This was around 66 BC, and set the stage early on for the involvement between the two men. Pompey saw nothing but victory in the East, and returned to a triumph in Rome. While revered as a great military hero, Pompey quickly learned that fighting political battles was going to be a much different conflict to wage than fighting military ones. His political reputation amongst his colleagues began to mirror that of Caesar's, which likely pushed them closer towards their inevitable alliance.

Pompey's most driving goal upon his return to Rome was to secure land for his veterans coming back with him from their Eastern victories. He had made a promise to them that he would procure land for them to live and farm on, now that he was dismissing his factions. At the time the Senate was run by the consulship of Cicero, an ally of Pompey's, but it was also littered with his antagonists as well. All of Pompey's land requests were put on hold, and the debates were delayed and extended. Pompey knew that the game of politics was to be played if he wanted to get anything done, and he would need to seek out more contentious strategies if he was to circumvent this authority which was weighing down on him. The political climate practically made secret alliances a necessity, and Pompey found his with Caesar, but not after compromising with the third party; Crassus.

Crassus had been a long time political rival of Pompey's, and this animosity is what Caesar used to form this alliance, honoring concerns of both men to secure his own growth in power. Crassus' legacy began with military prowess, much like Pompey. He had served under Sulla during his Roman Civil War, and after Sulla's victory Crassus found himself in a position of great potential, being so closely aligned with the man who had proven himself worthy by force to hold his office in Rome. When Sulla assumed control, his proscriptions took out his anger on his victims in every way Sulla could think of. One such strategy was selling off the property of his enemies for dirty cheap, desecrating the image of his opposition from the ground up. Crassus ingeniously exploited this and began buying up property left and right, effectively becoming one of history's earliest real estate moguls. In the years following the Roman Civil War, Crassus' wealth swelled to make him one of the richest men in history.

Having secured many lifetimes worth of fortunes, Crassus' main objective now was military exaltation. However, it was Pompey who would always be standing in his way of that fame which he pined for. Crassus played a large role in putting an end of Rome's most significant slave rebellion in all their history. It was the rebellion led by Spartacus, a household name to us now, whose been immortalized in books, television shows, and movies. Through graphic and ruthless leadership, Crassus drove Spartacus and his armies out of Rome with their tails between their legs. These scattered bands of forces were met by Pompey as they fled to the East, and it was

Pompey who, technically, wiped out the rebellion for good. However, it was obviously Crassus who played the bigger role in this conflict, yet Pompey took credit. Pompey would continue to take false credit for his involvement in conflicts, always looking to embellish the truth. He took a number of jabs at Crassus, effectively floundering his military reputation. The rivalry between Pompey and Crassus was alive and well, fueled by seemingly nothing more than greed and pettiness. Despite this, in 70 BC the two found themselves serving as consuls together.

When it comes to Julius Caesar, his connections to Crassus were through wealth, rather than military factors. Caesar made a plethora of political promises to Crassus in exchange for money. Caesar promised to oppose Pompey's policies and ideas, feeding on the bitter rivalry that existed between the two. He first sought this wealth during his run for Pontifex Maximus. It was Crassus' money that played a major role in getting Caesar elected in that position.

He called upon Crassus once again in 61 BC. Before he could leave to serve his governorship in

Hispania, Caesar's debts needed to be paid, or he could face exile. Crassus wasn't able to pay all of Caesar's debts, at he had accumulated many, but he contributed enough to allow Caesar safe passage out of Rome. Still though, Caesar couldn't risk becoming a private citizen, as remaining in political positions was the only thing keeping him safe from angry debt collectors. Consul was the position which would keep him safe and allow him to continue to subvert the law for his own gains, and with the support of two figures as prominent as Crassus and Pompey he knew he could win.

Through brilliant compromise, and an acute understanding of what everyone had to gain from the strategy, Caesar convinced Pompey and Crassus to set aside their rivalry and politically align themselves together with Caesar so that together they could push through all of their own initiatives, with each other's support thrown behind them. Caesar had already established his alliance with Crassus. Pompey was the one he would have to woo.

Pompey, in the midst of trying to secure farmland for his veterans, was easy to convince though. With the promise of this land, and any other issues Pompey might want to push through that didn't jeopardize the integrity of the other two triumvirates, Pompey was hooked. As some icing on the cake, Caesar married his daughter, Julia, to Pompey, securing the alliance on a political level, and now a familial one as well. With these three powerful men backing one another, their reach was wide, and their influence was deeply rooted in the system.

The election of 59 BC was an ugly one, to say the least. With their alliance firmly cemented, the triage of power that existed between Caesar, Crassus, and Pompey was unstoppable. The election campaign was rife with bribery and threats from all sides. The Triumvirate was being kept a secret from the rest of the Roman Senate, and Caesar was playing coy with where his wealth and sway was coming from. Ugly politics were no stranger in this climate, and the amount of backdoor maneuvering was basically commonplace.

Caesar ran against two opponents that year; Marcus Calpurnius Bibulus and Lucius Lucceius. The establishment was stacking the deck behind Bibulus, who ironically had already worked alongside Caesar before, serving as aedile with him many years prior. Lucceius had close ties with Cicero, who himself had ties with Pompey. A sort of mini-alliance was formed and Cicero's vast political and financial connections, combined with Crassus' overwhelming fortune, made the election a shoe-in for Caesar. He had hoped that his alignment with Lucceius would have procured the second consul seat for him, but with the financial aptitude of the ancient political elite behind him, Bibulus was able to swoop up that second seat. Caesar now found himself in an interesting position. The alliance had achieved what it was supposed to do, and its bigger goals of personal gain for the triumvirates were in a position to be set into motion. However, Bibulus was a wrench in these plans, as he would prove a major opposition to Caesar's policies.

Right out of the gate the establishment attempted to limit the power they knew Caesar was vigorously grabbing at. After serving a year long term, consuls become proconsuls in charge of governing assigned provinces. It is further opportunity for a consul to enact change and policy in lands outside of the direct Roman city. The power of proconsular was very legitimate, and the Senate immediately feared what Caesar could do with this power after his term was ended.

Thus, they delivered him a slap in the face by assigning him proconsular of, literally, just the forests and fields that lie on the outskirts of Italy. This, of course, wasn't going to stand for Caesar.

He employed the help of the incumbent consul, Lucius Calpurnius Piso Caesoninus to expand his proconsular governance to something actually substantial. This was a fairly easy favor to ask for Caesar, seeing as Piso was his father in law. In the winter of 59 BC Caesar had married Calpurnia, young Piso's daughter. This was admittedly a strange wedding, as Calpurnia at the time was younger than Caesar's own daughter, Julia. Caesar and Calpurnia would bare no children together, and it's not far fetched to say that this fact had something to do with it. At the time Julia had just married Pompey, weaving a tangled romantic web within the Caesares bloodline.

Nevertheless, these familial connections helped Caesar move his proconsulship from the outskirts of Italy, to the northern part of the country, otherwise known as Cispaline Gaul. His jurisdiction was expanded further to the West, to the area known as Illyricum, and finally

Transpaline Gaul was tacked on later. And, since this period of time was characterized by Caesar getting to have his cake and eat it too, his proconsulship term was extended to five years, rather than one, the norm for proconsuls. This accomplishment would provide the out that Caesar needed at the end of his term as consul, and a chance to escape prosecution once again.

. . .

The First Triumvirate had worked exceedingly well in its plot to get Caesar into power. The problem at hand now was making sure it kept working for the benefit of all three parties involved. Pompey's marriage to Julia was a wonderful consignment, but the real reason he was part of this triumvirate had not yet come to fruition, and it was a primary focus of Caesar's as he took office. Pompey was still waiting for the legal rights to land for the veterans of his Mithrandic conquests. For months Caesar toiled away on a land bill that was so meticulously drafted that he expected it draw little to no opposition. In a genuine moment of civility, Caesar made certain to craft an exquisitely fair bill. He made sure he was not personally connected to it in any way, and would see no sort of benefit from it. Everyone was appeased in his wording, and he came to the Senate confident in the bill's ability to pass.

Unfortunately, Caesar's optimate opposition, led primarily by Caesar's long time political rival Marcus Porcius Cato, was staunch. Caesar's fellow consul, Bibulus, was backed by Cato and company as well, and made it publicly known that he would stand against Caesar's proposition no matter what. So, in typical fashion, Caesar took matters into his own hands and went to the streets. He advocated the significance of the bill directly to the people, appeasing the common man sensibilities that his image upheld. He used Bibulus' unwavering opposition to the bill against him, painting the image of a self-serving hedonistic Senate who only thought of themselves in their legislation. This was an image that certainly riled the feathers of Caesar's supporters, along with the common Roman citizen.

With the impassioned support of the people behind them, the First Triumvirate decided to go public. Pompey and Crassus both declared their adamant support of Caesar's bill, and the power of the trio was made known. The Senate already viewed Caesar as a force to be reckoned with, but now that they knew he had the support of one of the greatest military generals of the time, and quite possibly the richest man on earth, the magnitude of his capabilities intensified. A fire was lit under Bibulus and his party, and in sordid efforts they attempted to denounce Caesar and his alliance, throwing everything they could at him, but were circumvented by Caesar once again.

Caesar employed his powers as Pontifex Maximus to decree any opposition of the bill to be null, and to invoke a relocation of the bill's vote. He transferred the vote to the Temple of Castor where a public forum was held. By this time Caesar had garnered overwhelming public support, and there was little the Optimates could do to stop this momentum. Bibulus arrived at the Temple in a last ditch effort to stop the bill, but was met with grotesque hostility. He was booed and jeered out of the Temple, and on his way down the steps someone dumped a bucket of poop on his head. Who's to say if it was human poop, or the feces of farm animals, but the message was very clear to Bibulus and the rest of the

Optimate party that their way of running things was no longer going to be accepted by the general populace.

      Bibulus was disgraced, and with the Optimates losing control of the Senate, he had little power in the halls of the forum, and abandoned his post to return home to end his term as a lame duck consul. Throughout the rest of the year he made fairly pitiful efforts to denounce what Caesar was doing as consul, but they were always in vein, and only desecrated his reputation further. By the end of 59 BC Bibulus was a joke, and that year would later come to be known as the consulship of Julius and Caesar, a fitting name for a year that gave the Roman people only a taste of what Caesar's political connections and public charisma could get him.

.   .   .

As consul, Caesar's public image was of major concern to him, as this image was everything if he was to continue building this momentum of support that was amassing around him in the general population. Caesar's knack for manipulation was exemplified here. He recognized how imperative the propaganda machine was, a truth that remains ever relevant today. Caesar knew this was a machine that had to be turning its wheels at all times, constantly and, more importantly, consistently shaping his public notoriety to be where he wanted it to be. His first concrete step in doing so was enacting into law a bill that stated all debates and Senatorial procedures must be made public. This bill would help the transparency of his advocacy, showing the public who he fought for on the steps of that sacred building.

Throughout his consulship Caesar continued to tickle the fancy of his fellow triumvirates. He proposed tax bills which greatly benefited Crassus and his business interests. Pompey's territory to the East continued its expansion. Caesar continued to take bills to the people's assembly, cutting out his use of the Senate. He saw great success in passing laws which filled Crassus' pockets, appeased Pompey's land ownership, and secured his own future as a military commander capable of unequivocal conquest.

Securing proconsulship of multiple Gallic territories was Caesar's last great victory in his year as consul, and it couldn't have come at a better time. Throughout a controversial and chaotic term as consul

Caesar had made a lot of enemies, and copious allegations of corruption had come to light. Shady political practices were beginning to catch up with Caesar, and he could see the prosecutor's hammer coming at him swiftly and heavily. In barely enough time, Caesar left Rome to head for Gaul. The appropriation of his five year imperator title gave him immunity from prosecution so long as he remained in his jurisdiction.

In one year as consul Caesar had drastically changed the political landscape of Rome, and he had shaken the Republic to its core. He expertly manipulated an already shaky system to serve his needs, constantly maintaining that lofty perspective which kept him outside of the law. Yet, even though that perspective caught up with him and brought him back down to Earth, it didn't matter. It only gave Caesar the chance for a change of course. What happened in 59 BC would be a launching point for a long and storied chapter of Caesar's greatest military conquests.

Chapter 5

The Gallic Wars

Upon leaving Rome, Caesar began his status as proconsul of Cisalpine Gaul and Illyricum. He also acquired Transalpine Gaul after Metellus Celer, the governor of the province, abruptly died. Caesar had the next five years laid out in front of him to expand his conquests and prepare himself for what kind of prosecution and scrutiny await him in Rome, if he ever wanted to return. With four legions backing him, Caesar looked to the northeast for potential conquest which could help him pay the debts which loomed over his potential political future.

The Gallic countries, while not as advanced as Roman civilization at the time, were nevertheless a civilized and organized society of people. The various tribes had plotted land allocations, and groups of tribes had even formed republics to maintain peace and stability in certain regions. Romanization was a fast spreading concept due to their geographically innovative influences like roads, and the culture had seeped into Gallic society.

As Caesar came to power in the territory, it had been a relatively peaceful time that was soon about to end. Rome enjoyed all degrees of financial and political relationships with the tribes of Gaul and maintained vital trade routes in the territories. It hadn't always been that way though. The history of the Romans and the Gallic tribes is a shaky one. Just fifty years prior, in 109 BC, Gallic tribes invaded Italy's northern border. Ironically, it was Caesar's uncle, Gaius Marius, who helped put an end to this invasion in violently gory conflict. Since this incursion, however, things had been relatively peaceful, with Rome limiting any invasive involvement with the region. All of this was about to change thanks to one ambitious military leader.

In recent years, the boat had begun to be rocked by Germanic tribes who were putting pressure on the Gallic tribes on their northern frontiers. Caesar had already been involved in these conflicts once, during his governance of Hispania. While in this position, a leader of the Germanic peoples named Ariovistus led a campaign into Gaul, plundering the border villages and causing violent uncertainty for the Gauls. Caesar nipped the situation by striking up an alliance with the Germans.

As Caesar considered his options, the current state of Gaul made it almost too enticing for him. Not only did its wavering politics and violent sensibilities pose a threat to Rome, giving him justification for warfare, it was also one of the most significant land grabs he could possibly undergo. The region was a rich resource center, with trade routes like the Rhone and the Rhine passing right through it. Conquering these territories would certainly mean an end to Caesar's debt issues, and all his actions would be validated.

And yet, while all this fortune was appealing to Caesar, it wasn't what pushed him the most. The fire inside him didn't burn for immense riches, it burned for immense glory. He pined for the military righteousness that he would achieve through such an expansive conquest of Central Europe. Caesar knew, no matter what, if he accomplished this, the name Julius Caesar would have its place cemented in history.

. . .

If, going in, Caesar didn't have enough of a reason to begin his military exploits in Gaul, 58 BC most certainly gave him that reason. In the northern region of Gaul, in what is now modern day Switzerland, a coalition of five different Gallic tribes, known together as the Helvetii, were finding themselves increasingly harassed by the Germanic tribes both in the north and the east. The Helvetii, led by Orgetorix, had made plans for a massive migration south. Their plan was to head towards Gaul's westernmost front, but to do so they would have to pass through territories where they feared they might not be welcome. One such territory was Transalpine Gaul, one of Caesar's provinces.

The Helvetii had a reputation for savagery in unmitigated migration, so Orgetorix took it upon himself to ensure their safe passage. He visited with the chieftans of the tribes whose land they would have to pass through, the Sequani and the Aedui. Orgetorix formed an alliance with Casticus and Dumnorix, the Sequani and Aedui chieftans, respectively. They made plans to gain total control of their tribes by the use of force, thus ruling the majority of Gaul between the three of them. However, their plan was thwarted when Orgetorix was found out and forced to stand trial. Before the trial, though, Orgetorix escaped and, through circumstances that remain unknown today, died. Caesar had his own assumptions, which presumed suicide.

Despite the death of Orgetorix, the Helvetii were still ready to undergo their migration, and Caesar was still ready to defend and use whatever force necessary. The Helvetii were quick to establish themselves as a force to be reckoned with. Some 370,000 men, women, and children departed the Helvetii lands, burning their own villages on the way out. This decimation ensured that they had no choice but to achieve what they had set out to do, and left nothing behind for their enemies to exploit.

When the Helvetii began their perilous march, Caesar was crossing the Alps, on his way to Illyricum, where he thought his command would be most needed. News of the Helvetii route, and its potential landing in Transalpine Gaul, spurred Caesar to turn right around and head for Geneva. He had only left one of his now six amassed legions there, a force that wouldn't stand a chance against the massive Helvetii army gaining momentum at every juncture. Upon arriving in Geneva

Caesar quickly gathered a group of auxillary troops to fortify the city's defenses.

Bloodshed was not the Helvetii's intent, and they sent requests for peaceful passage to Caesar. They assured Caesar that no force would be necessary if they were allowed through the city, but Caesar wasn't hearing it. He stalled any negotiations with the Helvetii, buying himself the time he needed to build him a unique defense for the time.

Caesar ordered the destruction of the bridge that went across the Rhone river, and provided the easiest passage into the city. He then had a rampart built, one that stretched nineteen miles across the outskirts of the city, A trench was dug parallel to the ramparts so that troops had easy and strategic passage for the major defensive effort that was about to be laid down. Caesar sent a brazen warning to the Helvetii that should any of them try and cross the Rhone, they would be met with the tip of a sword. The Helvetii underestimated Caesar's defensive strategy, and made numerous attempts to cross the river, all of which were met with just what Caesar promised. Caesar, along with his second in command,

Titus Labienus, successfully withheld the Helvetii attacks and forced them to turn around and rethink their strategy.

Just because the Helvetii had reversed their plunder, didn't mean they were no longer a threat, and Caesar knew this. As the Helvetii retreated to reopen their discussions with the Sequani and Aedui, Caesar set out of Cisalpine Gaul. He left Labienus in charge of Transalpine Gaul's legion, and began his mission to amass his forces in an offensive against the swelling Gallic threat.

With no time to lose Caesar took his army of five different legions through the Alps, encountering hostility along the way. He found himself involved in a number of skirmishes during his passage, but certainly caused more destruction than he endured. At the same time the Helvetii were engaged in a destructive spree across Gaul. They had pillaged the Aedui, the Ambarri, and the Allobroges tribes, who had sorely lacking defenses to put up against this faction of displaced and battle-ready legions.

The Helvetii certainly caused considerable destruction before they were finally met by Caesar and his army. As the Helvetii army crossed the river Arar, Caesar made his surprise attack. While most of the army had made it across the river, about a quarter of the Helvetii forces remained on the eastern front still waiting to cross. Caesar launched a brutal attack on them, and wiped out the majority of these forces, causing a crippling blow to the Helvetii offensive.

Caesar's pursuit of the Helvetii was in full force now, and nothing could stop it. A bridge was built across the river Arar so his forces could quickly gain ground on the army. For two nights Caesar led his hot pursuit, denying any claims for truce or reason the Helvetii attempted to send. The long winded pursuit took its toll on Caesar's forces, and after some ill advised maneuvers they lost their edge and had to concede the chase. Caesar marched them back towards Bibracte, an Aedui city. As soon as the Helvetii got wind of Caesar's retreat, they flipped the script and began their own pursuit.

With an upper hand, the Helvetii seemed to be gaining on Caesar, until he called for the legions of the two groups to face each other in formal battle. It was a bold move on Caesar's part, as he knew he was outnumbered and victory was by no means guaranteed. But despite the odds, the Battle of Bribacte would come to be known as one of his greatest victories.

The bloody battle raged on for nearly an entire day, and both sides saw dramatic losses. Caesar's forces waged an all-out slaughtering of Helvetii troops, eventually coercing their surrender, which Caesar rightfully accepted. The Helvetii began their expedition with over 350,000, and now Caesar was sending what was left of them back to their homelands. That remaining number was alarmingly small, as it is estimated around 100,000 people were left after the graphic campaign. The majority of their casualties were women and children, cannon fodder in the brutally indiscriminate first stage of the Gallic Wars.

. . .

While the Helvetii may have no longer been a threat to Gaul, a new threat was always there to take its place. This next force to shake the stability of the region was someone the Gaul's already had their experience with, but the tension was now headed towards a boiling point. Ariovistus, a Germanic king and chieftan of the Suebi tribe, was threatening Gaul's eastern front with invasion. Ariovistus had long been trying to secure more land for himself and his people through military victory and political influence. He threatened the integrity of both Gallic and Roman relations in the area, and was a force that could not be ignored.

Caesar was under pressure from the Gallic government to do something about this impending threat. The opportunity was beguiling to Caesar, given that conquering Ariovistus would mean expansion eastward, extending Rome's eastern borders. This would certainly put Caesar in good standing with politicians, civilians, and soldiers alike. There was an issue, however. To appease Ariovistus during his initial campaigns, Rome helped secure Ariovistus' stability and declared him a "king and friend of the Roman people." Caesar had no jurisdiction to declare war on the Suebi tribe, unless properly instigated. Caesar was most certainly looking for a fight when he demanded that Ariovistus halt his troops at the Rhine river. He threatened grave conflict should any German cross the river, and also demanded that Ariovistus remove himself from any involvement with the Aedui people, and their Aedui hostages be returned immediately. Ariovistus was done playing the negotiation game, though. He was not a man to sit idly by and play politics. He was a man of action, and refuted any opposition from Rome with force. His plan was to take what he felt he was entitled to by any means necessary. He was going to conquer because it was in his blood, and he knew it was in Caesar's blood, too.

Simultaneously, Ariovistus launched an attack on the Aedui by the Harudes, one of his allied clans, and began sending hundreds of his Suebi forces across the Rhine. Little did he know, he had just given Caesar exactly what he wanted. The grounds for war were cemented, and Caesar now had justification for mounting his offensive.

Ariovistus intended to make it to Vesontio, the largest Sequani city in the territory, and Caesar knew he had to make it there first. He did, prompting Ariovistus to request a truce. He requested they meet at a knoll to discuss this truce. During the discussions, Caesar got word of German horsemen creeping towards the knoll, harassing Caesar's military escorts. The truce was immediately called off. Stuck in a dire standstill, Ariovistus requested a second meeting just two days later.

This quick turnaround prompted appropriate hesitation from Caesar. Untrusting of the tactics Ariovistus was plotting, he sent two liaisons to represent him in the meeting, Valerius Procillus and Caius Mettius. Ariovistus saw this as a cowardly and detestable act, so he responded by imprisoning Procillus and Mettius. He then set out to intimidate Caesar, showing that he wouldn't stand for this kind of petty negotiation. He established camp two miles from Caesar's, effectively creating a communication and supply blockade for the Roman troops.

Caesar only took the shows of aggression with confidence, eagerly waiting for Ariovistus to make the first move, and jeopardize his encampment. In an attempt to prompt conflict, Caesar had a small camp erected closer to Ariovistus' position. This prompted just the effect Caesar hoped for when Ariovistus attacked the new camp, and was easily turned away. The morning after Ariovistus' failed insurgence, Caesar's forces lined up for an all encompassing offensive to bear down on Ariovistus and the Suebi. Caesar had distributed command of his legions to his five legates and his quaestor, and had organized an offensive from all sides to squash Ariovistus. It was another conflict that saw gallons of blood spilled upon the earth of Gaul, and it was another triumphant victory for Caesar. Ariovistus left with hardly any of his men still alive, and he would never threaten Rome again. It was perhaps the most concrete victory Caesar had yet to experience.

. . .

By the end of 58 BC Caesar had already seen two major victories in Gaul, and 57 BC would mark yet another. This time, Caesar was called upon to fight off the Belgae, a coalition of tribes who inhabited the regions around what is today Belgium. The Belgae had recently shown their own aggression against an allied Roman tribe, and were threatening their own killing spree. Caesar wanted to be certain of his strategy when facing these new opponents, and so he held his army back while awaiting intel about the Belgae's plans. Caesar was caught off guard when the Belgae didn't wait for a formal invitation to begin their conquest, and revealed their plans for domination pretty clearly to Caesar and his troops.

As they set up an encampment in proximity to the river Sambre, a massive legion appeared practically out of nowhere, and a devious sneak attack was launched on Caesar's army by the Nervii, one of the Belgae's most merciless tribes. The Nervii's attack was sudden and abrasive, and it was the closest Caesar had ever come to a defeat as he scrambled his troops together to flee the encampment. Legion X, or the 10th, Caesar's most honored legion of soldiers, made a valiant stand against the Nervii long enough for reinforcements to arrive. Caesar managed to amass a powerful defensive force that made short work of the descending Belgae tribes. The Artrebates and Viromandui tribes were quickly repelled, but it was the Nervii who persisted in the fight the longest. This warlike tribe fueled by savage bloodlust fought to their last man, with the bodies piling too high to even see over from ground level. Caesar quickly made the Belgae regret their offensive, and within the year he had burnt out any dissention in this region, and he took control of even more land.

With his Gallic conquests now gaining a reputation of bloodshed and brutality, Caesar struck fear into the hearts of any and all who opposed him in his territories. He made it his mission to expand Rome's territories, with a lust for imperialism catalyzing his actions. He sought anywhere that he might have grounds to squash rebellion or dissention. On Gaul's Atlantic border an anti-Roman confederacy was gaining traction between the Veneti and Armorica tribes. These seafaring tribes were equipped with a strong fleet and, even though Rome had little history of sea campaigns, Caesar amassed his own fleet and led a conquest against the coalition on both land and water.

When these tribes fell, Caesar, glowing with confidence, planned his next moves solely on egotistical domination of the world. Caesar had begun to underestimate his opponents, especially when he was met with absolutely zero conflict from the Suebi after crossing the Rhine in 55 BC. That same year, though, saw one of Caesar's most misguided displays of hubris. He led an expedition across the English Channel to wage war against the Britons, the ancient Celtic population that inhabited what stands as Great Britain now. Caesar was ill prepared for the sea expedition, especially when some nasty weather almost wiped out his entire fleet. Unable to regroup, Caesar withdrew this campaign, only to go back with a much bigger army the following year. In 54 BC Caesar enjoyed victory over Catuvellauni in Briton, and demanded that the country now pay its tribute to Rome. On the whole, these two years of campaigning would hold little political weight, and were really nothing more than a dramatic flashing of Caesar's power. It was clear that the purpose of Caesar's conquests had foregone monetary reasons, and he was now fueled by a desire to conquer.

.   .   .

Caesar's reach was shockingly far in the Gallic territories, especially considering how far he had gone and the history changing impact he had had in only a matter of years. Gaul was now a region under the steadfast control of the Roman Republic, and this came with major changes to their ways of life. Rome was a bustling empire that required considerable resources and payments from its territories to stay maintained. The Gauls had fairly inflammatory reactions to this subjugation, and in 53 BC uprisings began to occur. In North-Eastern Gaul a tribe called the Eburones amassed together to lead a campaign with the intent of driving out Roman influence. The campaign actually made some ground, and the Romans even came dangerously close to losing a strategic garrison. Caesar came to the rescue of the garrison, and launched a campaign against the Eburones. In order to show the rest of Gaul what happens to those who oppose Roman rule, Caesar's army hunted and practically wiped out the entirety of this unsuspecting tribe.

Apparently, though, Caesar's force wasn't crushing enough, as the Eburones uprising paled in comparison to the next great Gallic offensive, led by Vercingetorix of the Arveni tribe, a tribe of people who inhabited central Gaul. Vercingetorix called upon the Gallic people's dissatisfaction with their new rule, and encouraged them to stand up against the authority of Caesar, and take back their country. He launched what is known as a "scorched earth" campaign, dealing his biggest blows to his enemies supply line, focusing his attacks on resources rather than men. Caesar had to quickly mount his campaign against this threatening opposition. There was pushback and casualties on both sides, but eventually Vercingetorix was driven to the city of Alesia. Caesar launched a mighty siege on the city, effectively smoking out Vercingetorix and his army. As his forces ran out of food and supplies, the last remaining spirit of the Gallic forces fizzled out. Vercingetorix eventually had to secede his campaign and return from whence he came. His efforts were the last hurrah of the Gallic opposition, and his rebellion would be the last serious offensive the Gauls would launch against the Romans for the next two centuries.

Caesar had, it was safe to say, secured his victory of Gaul, and the Gallic Wars came to their conclusion with Caesar appropriately earning his reputation as a man of military cunning and conquest. His military strategy, unheard of at the time, secured him victories which should have been impossible. Any force daring enough to oppose Caesar now would be considered a band of fools. Caesar proved his aptitude outside of the Roman capitol but was about to called home once again.

Chapter 6

Caesar's Civil War

As Caesar led his unrelenting conquest across Gaul, he managed to only stay relatively involved in Roman politics. Upon leaving the city, Pompey and Crassus were the ones to stay behind to maintain the interests of the First Triumvirate. Upon Caesar's departure, however, the Triumvirate's power weakened significantly. It was discouraging, to say the least, for Pompey and Crassus to remain in Rome and weaken their grip on control of policy, while they meanwhile had to sit back and watch Caesar gain more and more fame and notoriety abroad. Roman politics were in peril as Publius Clodius Pulcher, a long time rival of Caesar and his supporters, was using unsavory tactics to get his policies around the authority of Pompey and Crassus. As Caesar's popularity and his campaign gained its momentum, Pompey and Crassus began to voice their concerns, and Caesar could feel the alliance shaking, something he couldn't afford to have happen.

In 56 BC Caesar called a secret meeting, called the Luca Conference, between him and his fellow triumvirs. They met in the city of Luca, Cisalpine Gaul's southernmost town that bordered on Italy's northern front. The meeting proved to be a success, as the strength of the First Triumvirate was reestablished through a new political strategy. It was agreed that both Pompey and Crassus would run for consul for the following year. With this position secured, all three men would gain extra benefit. First off, Caesar's proconsul duties in Gaul would be extended by five years. This is the provision which would allow him to continue and eventually conclude his Gallic Wars campaign. Pompey was promised the right to maintain his governorship of Hispania, a position he had procured at the conclusion of Caesar's consulship. He was granted the position *in absentia,* meaning he didn't have to be housed in Hispania for him to maintain his governance. This allowed him to stay in Rome after his consulship, and continue to play politics.

Finally, Crassus was appeased with the promise of his own governorship title over Syria. This was an incredibly valuable position, as Syria was the passageway to Parthia, a region yet unconquered by the Romans.

Crassus, likely inspired by Caesar's unabashed success in Gaul, had plans to invade Parthia, and takeover the Parthians, expanding Rome's borders and claiming the fame which he longed for, and was jealous of Caesar for.

Crassus, Pompey, and Caesar all returned from Luca highly confident of the years to come. This positivity was reinforced when in 55 BC Crassus and Pompey set in motion their plans and earned their positions as co-consuls. 55 BC was an uplifting and exciting year for the Triumvirate. The strength of the alliance had proven itself effective once again, and Caesar was able to maintain his grip on Roman politics without even being present. Of course, whenever plans seem to be going too well is when everything seems to come off the rails. Whatever stability and assuredness that was established in 55 BC came crashing down the following year.

In 54 BC Caesar and Pompey shared a mutually destructive loss. Julia, Caesar's daughter and Pompey's wife, was met with complications while giving birth to her and Pompey's child. Neither her or the baby survived. Pompey and Caesar were able to share in their sorrow, yet it was undeniable that a major contributing factor to the strength of their alliance was now out of the picture, and it would take its toll on their relationship.

The following year dealt an even bigger blow to a political alliance which was already coming apart at the seams. After the consulship of Pompey and Crassus, Crassus was left with governorship over Syria, something he was incredibly excited about given the implication of this geographical strongpoint. Upon taking command of the legions here, Crassus immediately began his campaign into Parthia, a fiery bloodlust in his eyes madly driving his thirst for conquest. Parthia was an incredible source of wealth and resources, and would have been a strategic land grab for the Republic, but this had little influence on why Crassus had his sights set there. It was the desire for fame, and a chance for his own conquests to rival what Pompey's military career had achieved, and what Caesar was currently achieving in Gaul. Crassus was dangerously eager to find success in Parthia, and this drove him to making dire mistakes.

King Artavazdes II of Armenia had extended a hand to Crassus, offering him almost forty thousand troops if Crassus would agree to attack from Armenia and

Parthia's shared border. In a regrettable display of ego, Crassus declined Artavazdes' offer and instead opted for the direct route across the Euphrates. Crassus' campaign began in 54 BC, and saw its swift ending the following year in Carrhae. The Battle of Carrhae saw a relatively small Parthian force wipe out nearly all of Crassus' soldiers. As Crassus' forces were slaughtered before him he refused to do anything but stand his ground, convinced that the onslaught of Parthian arrows barreling down upon would eventually run dry. His men, in adamant opposition to this plan threatened mutiny, yet before any sort of counter-offensive could be mounted Crassus was finally overtaken, and lost his own life during his final stand against the Parthians.

One third of the Triumvirate was dead, thanks only to hubris and hastily poor decision making on the battlefield. In a bid for global conquest and fame, Crassus had sent himself to his own death, ending his life as an overzealous fool. The Triumvirate was in absolute shambles, with Crassus dead and the relationship between Pompey and Caesar becoming dangerously rocky. In 52 BC Caesar made one final attempt to at least keeping his relationship with Pompey afloat. Knowing the importance of a marital alliance, Caesar offered his grandniece, Octavia, to Pompey as his next wife. However, Pompey refused. Instead, he married Cornelia Metella, the daughter of Caecilius Metellus Scipio, a man who had been a political rival of Caesar's for many years now. Who's to say if Pompey had any sort of emotional interest in Cornelia. This move was likely nothing more than a very clear message to Caesar that their alliance was over, and the Triumvirate could be considered as dead as Marcus Licinius Crassus.

.   .   .

The end of the First Triumvirate was met with a tumultuous turn in Roman politics. Pompey's allegiance was now shifting back towards the Optimates, and he found himself in alignment with Cato, someone who could possibly be considered Caesar's longest running political rival. Caesar's reputation with his home city was incredibly polarizing at this point. The people of Rome revered Caesar. He was a war hero, a conqueror, and a representative of the people's interests. The Senate was a different story. Caesar's friends in the Forum were slowly dwindling. Two tribunes, Mark Antony and Quintus

Cassius Longinus, remained loyal to him, but a Cato led Optimate opposition, now with the force of Pompey behind them as well, was fearful of the power and notoriety which Caesar had amassed through his campaign of Gaul.

With the Triumvirate officially disbanded, Pompey took sole consulship of Rome in 52 BC. Caesar was wrapping up the Gallic Wars at the time, stomping out the last rebellious Gauls who thought it wise to oppose their new Roman citizenship. Of course, his gaze was turning back towards Rome, specifically vying for the position of consul once again. By regaining this position, Caesar could use his newly acquired influence to push his agenda that much further. More importantly, however, having a secure position as consul awaiting him on his return to Rome would keep Caesar safe from prosecution once more. This threat loomed ominously before Caesar left for Gaul, given his less than ethical practices during his first consulship, but now they loomed with an even more dire dread. Caesar's campaigns through Gaul weren't exactly approved by the Senate, a protocol that all military generals before Caesar had followed to a tee. Caesar's campaign, in his mind, went above the well wishes of the

Roman Senate. This was for himself, and securing his own name in history, which he obviously accomplished. Caesar's opponents were ready to tear him apart for the atrocities committed during this illegal campaign.

The Senate was rightfully fearful of a consul who commanded an army the likes of which Caesar had banded together for one of the history's greatest military crusades. They demanded he give up all command of his army if he did not want to face prosecution and potential force. Caesar agreed to do so on one condition. Pompey was to do the same. The Senate took offence to Caesar's bold requests and doubled down on their demands. Caesar was to relinquish command of his arm, or he would be declared an enemy of Rome, and any attempt of his to enter the city would be met with force. They also worked to shut down his political momentum, denying him any ability to run for consul *in absentia.*

Caesar was of course not about to give up command of the army which had carried him through so many victories. He wasn't about to dump this power and this strength, and the bonds which he had created with these men who braved truly horrific conflict. He amassed his army in Cisalpine Gaul, ready for what was to come. Marcus Antonius, a friend and cohort of Caesar's colloquially named Mark Antony, along with Cassius joined him there after their exile from Rome. They had sworn their allegiance to Caesar, and were cast from the Senate when they attempted to stop Pompey's plans to strip Caesar of his army.

Caesar's strength was put on glorious display as he rallied vehement distaste of the Senate amongst his army. He inspired them to turn against the establishment, and to stand with him as he took back the government for the people of Rome. He had the support of regular Roman citizens lifting him up, and he knew that any action he took against the political elites would be met with reverence by the common people. He was prepared for anything, hoping to solve the situation politically, but more than willing to enact force if need be.

As Caesar's proconsulship came to its official end he was faced with having to make the decision. He could either disband his army and enter Rome as a private citizen, which would immediately be met with a barrage of prosecution, and his political career could likely come crashing down, never to regain what it once had. His other option was to keep his army, enter Rome, and take care of these political quarrels himself. On January 10th, 49 BC, Caesar chose the latter option.

Once crossing into Rome, there would be literally no turning back, and Caesar would be officially declared a public enemy by the Senate. This made his January 10th crossing of the Rubicon River, his finest legions filling the ranks behind him, one of the most decisive and historical moments of all Roman history. It marked the beginning of a brutal Civil War that Caesar would rage against his political opposition for years to come.

. . .

Caesar's crossing of the Rubicon definitively set in stone his intent, and that no power on Earth was above him. Civil war had begun, and Pompey quickly realized the calamitous ramifications of this. He declared that "Rome cannot be defended," and fled to Capua, an Italian city further south from Rome, along with the rest of the Optimate party. It was a move of utter cowardice that only proved the threat Caesar posed. Caesar made sure to capitalize on this crippling display of weakness, and continue marching south towards the city.

Pompey was no useless coward though. Despite his knee-jerk flee from Rome, he was doing all he could to gather his own forces to mount a defense against Caesar's bloody momentum. He put together two legions comprising of nearly 12,000 soldiers, and also gained the assistance of a band of Italian forces led by Lucius Domitius Ahenobarbus. Pompey dispatched Domitius and his army towards Massilia, hoping to cut Caesar off on his path to Rome from the direction of the Adriatic seaboard. Pompey himself took his army and fled even further south. They set off for Brundisium, a peninsula city in southern Italy, where he and his army could find transport by sea to reach Epirus, a Roman controlled Greek province to the East. The Optimates regathered their bearings in Brundisium, with Cato and Metellus joining Pompey at the city.

Caesar was not concerned with conquest in this conflict, and only aimed for some kind of compromise to bring the fighting to an end. He implored Pompey to lay down his sword so that the two could discuss the matter at hand. Regardless of the shaky relationship which had pulled Caesar and Pompey through so many tumultuous circumstances, Caesar didn't want to end his relationship with Pompey through hostility. He wanted to salvage what they had accomplished previously, and agree to peaceful terms. Caesar's placidness didn't resonate with Pompey though. Pompey only chose to highlight Caesar's insubordination, and took the unemotional stance that Caesar was legally an enemy of the state, and that he had a military obligation to forcefully defend against this onslaught.

Caesar was making his fast approach of Brundisium, with a mutual understanding between him and Pompey that war was now the only option. Pompey and the rest of the Optimates narrowly escaped the city, evading Caesar again, and prompting him to redirect his pursuit. Caesar looked for vulnerability amongst the Roman provinces, and his next strategic point to intercept. Caesar put his legions in reverse, and they made their way north once again, towards Hispania. Pompey was still governor of the province, but he was obviously preoccupied with his escape to Epirus. This left Pompey's massive legions lying in wait under the command of Lucius Afranius and Marcus Petreius, two of Pompey's closest legates. Victory awaited for whoever could gain the edge in Hispania, and Caesar was determined to do so, and dissipate Pompey's army.

Upon leaving Brundisium, Pompey had dispatched Domitius to the city of Massilia to stir up opposition to Caesar. Caesar was to pass through Massilia to reach Hispania, but was met with closed gates. Caesar launched a siege of the city, complete with siege towers and battering rams, yet the Massiliots mounted an incredible defense. This proved a major setback for Caesar's advancement. His strategy was thrown for a loop, and he left Gaius Trebonius and Decimus Junius Brutus Albinus to lead the siege. He himself pressed onward to Hispania Citerior, where three legions were currently heading themselves to provide reinforcements at the Hispania border.

When he arrived, Caesar wasted no time in making his move on Hispania. He and his legions crossed the border and began their march into the province. Pompey's army, currently lacking the leadership of Pompey himself, had established a campsite on a hill near the city of Illerda. Caesar came threateningly close to the Pompey encampment, setting up his own camp spitting distance from his enemies. This hill was the strategic chokepoint of this ensuing battle, which was more of a series of skirmishes and a back and forth quarrel for geographical control, than it was a battle per se.

The campaign lasted for a lengthy amount of time with both parties instigating conflict, with little ground to gain. Eventually, Caesar made a significant offensive move, building a bridge over the river Sicoris to overtake Petreius and Afranius' camp. They fled in order to meet up with another troop farther inland, but Caesar's pursuit was swift. He overwhelmed the army's rear guard, and cut off the Pompeian retreat. The pressure gauge was bordering on explosion as the two armies made camp alarmingly close to one another yet again. Caesar had managed to set up on three sides of Pompey's army, and just needed to push them back a little further to finish the job. With one more offensive, Pompey's forces were pushed back, retreating further towards Illerda. Petreius and Afranius were completely surrounded at this point, and had no point but to admit defeat.

Caesar's legate, Cassius, was left in Hispania to command the legions there as Caesar pressed on to wrap up Hispania. The legions in Hispania Ulterior immediately conceded and Hispania was under Caesar's control once more. He had dealt his most significant blow yet to Pompey, who was knowing some successes in his campaigns against Caesar's army in places like Africa, but was slowly cracking under the weight of Caesar's onslaught.

On his return from Hispania, Caesar made a stop at Massilia to finish the siege. The Massiliots had maintained an admittedly honorable defense against Caesar's forces, even sneakily destroying the siege machinations of Caesar's army under cover of darkness. Ultimately, however, the city had to concede when Caesar returned with new accomplishments under his belt. They admitted defeat and opened their gates to Caesar and his army. He showed mercy and didn't stop Domitius' attempt to flee, and allowed the city of Massilia to remain in good standing with the Romans.

Caesar's civil war, though bloody and lengthy, was having Caesar's desired effect. He had scattered the

Optimate Senate and sufficiently broken their ranks hard enough to return to Rome. With the Optimate rule in disarray, Roman politics were ripe for the taking. So ripe, in fact, that they were basically handed to Caesar when Marcus Lepidus nominated him to take command of Rome as its dictator, a controversial move with mixed results. Obviously, Caesar accepted the position and returned to Rome. He claimed his seat as dictator, and named Mark Antony his Master of the Horse, the lieutenant position to all Roman dictators. His mission now was to restore some semblance of stability amongst the shattered Roman Senate, and end the surge of conflict that had erupted from his civil war. Fighting was going on all across Roman territory, some confrontations ending better than others. Pompey and Cato stood as Caesar's greatest threats, and the issues that would have to be dealt with sooner rather than later. Curio, one of Caesar's legates, had already ran an embarrassingly unsuccessful campaign against the Optimates in Africa, where they were allied with King Juba of Numidia. The ill advised offensive against Publius Attius Varus and his solidly amassed legions was a disaster that led to Curio's death, and prompted major pressure for Caesar to bring this war to a close.

Within eleven days Caesar ended his dictatorship after using the time to smooth tensions on the home front. Peace was not an option as long as the new Roman Senate's enemies were still in operation, and Caesar knew he had to turn right around and leave Rome once again to once again lead a pursuit of Pompey. Caesar's Civil War had torn Rome apart, and he was determined to put it back together. Little stood in his way, but what was obstructing this peace were two serious forces to be reckoned with. Caesar knew that if this Civil War was to come to a close, both Pompey and Cato would have to be defeated.

Chapter 7

Old Enemies and New Allies

Pompey was the top priority for Caesar, as he longed to end this feud with a man whom he was once able to call colleague, son in law, and maybe even friend. But while Caesar was busy stamping out Pompey's armies in Hispania, Pompey was amassing a fresher, tougher, and more sizeable force for himself in Macedonia. Pompey's tenacity had allowed him to motivate an army, recruited mainly from maritime towns. Pompey's forces had sweeping control of the Adriatic Sea, and Caesar's plan was to cross it. With a magnanimous army of twelve legions, he left Rome and set out for Brundisium.

Getting to this port city was the easy part, it was crossing the Adriatic that would be the more perilous, and not just because of Pompey's grip on the waters. Caesar was arriving in Brundisium late in the year, and the wintery conditions made safe passage across the waters uncertain for anyone who dared take the journey. Of course, this fact was part of Caesar's strategy, assuming his enemies wouldn't suspect anyone to set out across the Adriatic at this time of year. Caesar had a problem much bigger than the weather to deal with though. An all too familiar face was the commander of Pompey's fleet that stood between Caesar and his rival. Marcus Calpurnius Bibulus, Caesar's co-consul who was embarrassingly run out of the Senate, had been appointed commander of Pompey's wickedly powerful fleet of ships, and now he was the most significant thing standing in Caesar's way. Buckets of dung wouldn't do the trick this time.

As icing on the cake, none of these matters were made any better by the fact that Caesar and his army didn't actually have a fleet of their own. Nothing was guaranteed for Caesar as he entered Brundisium, but he was resourceful. He managed to secure a fleet, but it wasn't enough to transport his entire army in one trip. Seven legions would be able to depart with Caesar, but the other five would have to remain in Brundisium, and await the fleet's return. As 49 BC approached its close, Caesar set out across the Adriatic, while Mark Antony stayed behind to command the remaining legions.

Much to Caesar's satisfaction, his crossing of the Adriatic went off without a hitch. Despite the choppy waters and inclement weather, it was an uneventful crossing, and after arriving at Palaeste, Caesar's fleet began its return journey. Unfortunately, however, the ease of Caesar's first crossing came with a catch. The journey had taken enough time for Bibulus to catch wind of Caesar's plan. He discovered the fleet's route, and intercepted them, burning the majority of the ships. Bibulus had gotten to enjoy at least an inkling of revenge against his tormenter, and now Caesar's passage was blocked. Without means to transport Mark Antony, the five remaining legions, or a significant amount of the army's resources, Caesar found himself in dire straits.

Caesar's options were scarce, as he no way of getting the rest of his men to him, and no chance of being helped by Greece, where Pompey had already garnered unwavering support. Battle was Caesar's only option, and he knew he would have to brave rough waters, figuratively and literally. As Caesar's armies scrounged for supplies, they also took the initiative to disturb Pompey's fleet, attacking ports and taking hard hitting swings against Pompey's supply lines. They managed to cut off resources to Bibulus and his fleet, and he eventually succumbed to illness, and when he died Lucuius Scribonius Libo took charge of the fleet.

Eventually, Caesar mustered up the resources and the confidence to attempt a daring return mission to Italy. Fearing his vulnerability on the Eastern side of the Adriatic sea, Caesar thought it best to return to Rome and make his army whole again. This plan didn't go accordingly though, and rough weather conditions managed to keep Caesar and his fleet where they were.

On the other side of the Adriatic, Mark Antony and his division of the army were amassing their own strength, to do what they could against the blockade which kept him from Caesar. After multiple attempts, Antony caught a bout of luck and overcame Libo's blockade. Strong wind currents set them off course though, and rather than heading straight for Caesar's location, they were redirected north, and would be landing near the city of Lissus. Both Caesar and Pompey were informed of Antony's success, and it was suddenly a race to meet him at his landing point.

Pompey and Caesar were equally determined to reach Antony, and they both made out on hot pursuit. Pompey managed to gain significant ground on Caesar, and surpassed his army, making it to Antony first. However, Caesar was not far behind, and Pompey concluded that he would be better off detracting from this pursuit, or he would risk being pinned in between both armies, a surefire path to obliteration. Pompey's choice was easy and he made a quick redirect in the direction of Dyrrachium, an incredibly strategic seafront town.

Dyrrachium lie on the northern tip of the Adriatic Sea, and it was both an able bodied stronghold and a major shipping port. Resources abounded in Dyrrachium, and it was in Pompey's best interest to secure a base of operations here. Pompey narrowly escaped being sandwiched by two devastating forces, but it didn't matter to Caesar. He was joyous to be reunited with Mark Antony and the rest of his legions. It had taken longer than expected, but Caesar's entire and unequivocally mighty army was across a body of water thought impossible to cross at this time, and he was ready to bring down his might of twelve legions on Pompey.

Caesar marched his army to Dyrrachium, but found it to be a huge risk to launch an all out siege upon the fortified city. Caesar revisited his strategies from the Gallic Wars, and built fortifications outside of the walls of Dyrrachium. Pompey's back was up against the sea, which was incredibly convenient for the purpose of supplies, but not so convenient when an army of twelve legions is ominously looming outside the city walls. Pompey decided to have his own fortifications built, and the battlegrounds for this conflict became the relatively small strip of land between the garrisons of the two armies. The configuration created a stalemate between the two, with neither side seeing any progress result from the daily skirmishes.

As the siege wore on for months, claustrophobia began to weigh on Pompey. Being able to resupply via the port was invaluable to Pompey's efforts, but he was simply running out of land to maintain the resources he was receiving. He was going to have to make moves, and get his army out of the standstill that was persisting outside the city. Caesar had enough land to cultivate for his armies sustainment, and time was not nearly as pressing on his side of the battle. Pompey was breaking, and it was time to take an offensive if he was going to keep from shattering.

With the help of outside intelligence Pompey found a weak spot in the fortifications Caesar had erected. The southern end of the wall was still under construction, and was vulnerable to an attack. Pompey knew he had to take advantage of this only temporary weakness in Caesar's defenses, so he called upon six legions to march out and exploit it. Pompey's troops brought a brutal fight to Caesar's 9th legion, stationed at that end of the wall, and managed to push them back. Caesar quickly mounted a defense which managed to cut short Pompey's attack and expel his forces. Caesar's quick and battle ready intellect had managed him many victories over insurmountable odds, but the stars were not aligned for this one. Pompey's army was simply too large, and Caesar's army found itself outnumbered to a dangerous degree. Caesar did all he could to hold his position as Pompey barreled down upon him. Pompey had been busy recruiting all throughout his land, and had secured allies in all different directions. This never ending onslaught finally caused a break in Caesar and he had no choice but to undergo a full-fledged retreat. In a disorderly and sloppy fashion Caesar's crippled army fell back from Pompey after undergoing heavy losses.

Even Pompey himself was shocked that he was witnessing a Caesarian retreat. His shock came with skepticism, and he neglected to pursue Caesar in his retreat, fearful of a trap. Even in defeat, Caesar was an unpredictably threatening opponent who kept his enemies on their toes, and this reputation likely saved his life. Caesar said of this turn of events, "Today the victory had been the enemy's, had there been any one among them to gain it." Pompey had a prime opportunity to end this civil war swiftly, but decided against it, and would have to regroup and continue the fight.

.   .   .

Caesar's retreat led him to Gomphi, another quaint seaside town that Caesar quickly overtook and exploited for the restocking of his army. After such a long and harrowing campaign of crossing and re-crossing tumultuous seas, and waging a frustratingly back and forth siege, Caesar was growing weary of the cat and mouse tactics their armies were employing. He was ready for planned combat, in the open, with both armies facing each other, ready to fight to the death. Pompey was not akin to this idea, preferring instead to loom just outside of the borders of Caesar's army, in an attempt to starve them out. However, emotions were running rampant within Pompey's camp, and his accompanying Senators were longing for sweeping and uncontested victory over Caesar. They pressured Pompey into accepting Caesar's request to do battle on the plains of Pharsalus.

    The entirety of Caesar's military might was staring down the combined strength of the forces that Pompey had been able to muster all across the Eastern provinces. Caesar was outnumbered, but had put faith in his own tact, and the intellect of his commanders. Pompey posted up and stood his ground on the field, prompting Caesar to mount his advance towards them. When the armies met face to face, roaring battle ensued and both sides fought valiantly. Pompey's much larger cavalry was able to overtake Caesar's cavalry, yet played into Caesar's hands by doing so when they were surprised by a hidden fourth line in Caesar's formations.

    Pompey's cavalry was dealt a mighty blow, and their integrity crumbled quickly. At this point Caesar launched his all out assault on Pompey's camp, sending in every one of his soldiers for a brutal charge on the scattered forces of Pompey's army. All Pompey could do was watch as his army was slaughtered before his eyes, something he knew would happen in this kind of engagement, yet went through with it anyways. Pompey had had enough of this war which seemed like it could rage on forever, and so he abandoned his forces entirely. He dropped his general's coat, gathered his family and what wealth he had and relinquished his own command of what was left of his totally spent forces. Pompey was done with military life, and sought only refuge from any sort of involvement with Caesar or his relentless civil war. He assumed, due to his popularity in the East, that Egypt, under the rule of the twelve year old King Ptolemy XIII, would be a safe haven.

Caesar came in to clean up what Pompey had abandoned and finished off the last of Pompey's brave defenders. It was one of Caesar's most impeccably stupendous military victories, in which he sustained hardly any losses compared to the epic scale of the battle. It was also an unquestionable victory over one of Caesar's greatest military adversaries.

．　　．　　．

The Battle of Pharsalus stomped out much of Caesar's opposition, and this victory saw a major shift in the civil war. The senators which had opposed Caesar were mostly either dead now, or had fled to other continents, looking to remove themselves from this brutally unrelenting political system. Pompey was no longer a threat to Caesar, but he did want to find him and pardon him so that their conflict could finally be put behind them, and he could officially concede. Caesar arrived at the Egyptian kingdom of Alexandria in September of 48 BC to find Pompey, but the condition in which he found him was far from what he had expected.

Caesar's conquests had obviously earned him a more admonished reputation than Pompey's, because when Pompey arrived to Egypt he was almost immediately murdered, an order given by King Ptolemy. Caesar was presented with Pompey's head, a sight which brought him to tears. After such vicious battles, Caesar was truly hoping to move on and give Pompey the recognition and respect in Rome which Caesar genuinely thought was deserved. Instead, Pompey was dead, and

Caesar was beginning to see an enemy in the young Ptolemy.

. . .

The politics of Egypt in recent years had been equally, if not more unstable than the situation in Rome. Caesar arrived to the country at a time of considerable unrest, and saw an opportunity. He took it upon himself to handle the current issue of who would and should rule Egypt, obviously wanting to put in power whoever would have his own best interest in mind. Obviously Ptolemy was not this option. With little resistance Caesar took over Alexandria and assumed temporary control. His options were limited, that was until a woman arrived to the city, smuggled in with bedsheets, that would change Caesar's life forever.

Cleopatra VII was Egypt's other potential heir to the kingdom, but given her storied past was not in a position to claim this title without the help of somebody with more strength under his command. Cleopatra was the sister of Ptolemy, and had recently been ousted from her position as Queen of Egypt. Through intriguing circumstances, Cleopatra had come to own that power at only 17, after the death of her father, Ptolemy XII. Her and her brother assumed a joint-rule of the country, technically, but Cleopatra essentially dismissed the will of her brother, and had assumed total control of Egypt around the time Caesar's civil war was getting into full swing.

Egypt possessed a long history of debts to the Romans, and had, for centuries, been in the Republic's debt. When the civil war broke out, Cleopatra was obligated to support Rome, and aid Pompey's army any way that was requested of her. Cleopatra, much like Caesar, had made a lot of enemies amongst her country's wealthy elite, and they were itching for a chance to expel her from the throne. Her quick bending to the will of the Roman's was just the excuse they needed, and Cleopatra was forced from power and exiled from Egypt. Cleopatra had little choice in the matter, with both the aristocracy and the citizens of Egypt calling for her banishment.

Cleopatra had gathered an army together in Arabia and Palestine, and had intended to march back towards Egypt to reclaim the throne from her younger brother. As she began her march, though, word reached her of Pompey's defeat. Part of her plan hinged on Pompey's success and momentum, but now that was over. Of course, no military ally was quite as valuable as the likes of Julius Caesar, so Cleopatra's alternative wasn't so bad. She managed to sneak into Alexandria and conduct a private meeting with him.

While there is a lot of speculation about what occurred in this great meeting of two unbelievably important historical figures, there are certain things easy to assume. One is that Cleopatra didn't just use her charm and vernacular to win the support of Caesar. Nine months after their meeting she bore their child, and long before that major plans went into motion to change the political landscape of Egypt forever.

Cleopatra proved herself to be the most viable political asset Caesar could possess in the East, and they could both benefit from what each other had if she was to assume power over Egypt once again, and his reign of Rome was to continue. Not to mention the fact that Cleopatra was absolutely enticing to Caesar. She was a powerful and persuasive woman, the likes of which Caesar had never known within male dominated Roman politics. She represented something greater than politics though, and was held in great reverence amongst her religious supporters. If Caesar was to become a God of Rome, it only made sense for him to align himself with the Goddess of Egypt.

Their bond was formed that night over sweat, flesh, and lust, but it was a bond that had greater political implications than Caesar could have ever predicted. Caesar had made his decision on who he would place in power, and when Ptolemy found out he was distraught. He attempted to flee the palace but was captured. Caesar had declared his animosity towards Egypt's current rule, and he and his relatively small force prepared themselves for battle, as the Egyptian general Achillas fortified himself outside Alexandria's walls and prepared to attack.

The Egyptian plan was to bare down hard on Alexandria, and smoke Caesar and his forces out of the city. They went for Caesar's supply line first, attacking the harbor in an attempt to render Caesar's resupplying and escaping impossible. The defensive edge allowed Caesar's men to retain control of the harbor, and the Egyptian fleet was viciously burned in their retreat. Caesar's inferno of a defense was unkempt, though, and the fire spread into the city, doing unbiased damage to both sides. Perhaps the saddest loss that occurred in the flames of Alexandra was The Great Library. It is depressing to think of the extent of historical literature that succumbed to those flames, but such is the immeasurable cost of war.

About a month into the siege, Caesar's ground only consisted of the palace and the harbor. Achillas assumed control of the city itself. Caesar's greatest asset at the moment was who he had with him in that palace. Obviously Cleopatra stood firmly by his side, as the entangled lovers had made their decision and there was no turning back from the conflict raging on the outside of the palace walls. They still had Ptolemy in their possession as well, along with Cleopatra's younger sister, Arsinoe IV. This latter leverage wouldn't last, though, because Arsinoe, with the help of her tutor and mentor Ganymedes, managed to escape and rejoin the Egyptian forces.

Achillas was confident in his insistent assault on the city, but Arsinoe thought differently. She was worried about Achillas' leadership and where his ego would take him in this siege. He had already proclaimed himself Pharaoh by his own decree, and would hear none of the insight from Ganymedes, somebody Arsinoe obviously had a lot of faith in. Arsinoe had Achillas executed, and Ganymedes assumed control of the Egyptian army.

Under new leadership, the Egyptian army turned up the heat on Caesar and his dwindling forces inside the palace. He knew that reinforcements were going to be necessary, and called for relief from some of Pompey's former legions, which he now had command over. As Ganymedes dealt blows to Caesar's supply of fresh water, his situation looked grim. Pompey's former legions, led by Calvinius, showed up just in time and gave Caesar's army the size and intimidation needed to meet the Egyptian fleet for battle. An estimated sixty ships, thirty on either side, met on the waters of the Mediterranean. Caesar emerged victorious in this aquatic skirmish, and continued his pursuit of the Egyptians to Pharos, a small fortified island. This may have been an overextension on Caesar's part, as the ensuing conflict here resulted in the decimation of many of his ships. Caesar's own vessel was sunk, and he had to swim to the safety of another ship.

With every sunken ship, though, the Roman legions fought even harder and without mercy. Ganymedes read the message loud and clear that the Romans had no plans of pulling back their offensive, forcing him to undergo a retreat. Little still had changed in the battle's power struggle. Caesar maintained his hold on the palace and surrounding harbors, while Ganymedes posted back up in the city. The stalemate continued.

More months passed, and by December both sides were getting discouraged. They had both been tattered and beaten down, yet neither side had any advantage over the other. The fighting had grown weary, and it stopped altogether when peaceful discussion between the two factions commenced. They eventually came to the agreement that Caesar would release Ptolemy in return for Egypt's sworn allegiance to Rome. They would retain their independence, but would live under the pretenses of Roman civilization. The agreement seemed all too promising as Ptolemy safely exited the palace to return to his people. This would end up being the last time Caesar ever trusted the Egyptians, because once Ptolemy reunited with his army the siege immediately started back up.

The idea of stalemate was driven in ever deeper, as now virtually nothing had changed in this war, other than the location of Ptolemy. Neither side could gain any sort of advantage, and Caesar realized that the only way to bring an end to this draining conflict was help from outside the city walls. This wasn't a problem for the most well connected military leader of the era. Mithridates of Pergamum, a military ally of Caesar's with no relation to Pompey's long time Grecian adversary King Mithridates, was building an army to come and relieve Caesar's forces.

The year was 47 BC by the time Caesar had his resources and strategy aligned well enough to mount one last final push against the Egyptians. Mithridates was marching towards Alexandria with forces he had gathered in Syria, and Ganymedes had no choice but to pull his strength back from the palace to deal with the fast approaching reinforcements. Caesar followed closely behind. Ptolemy and Ganymedes laid siege upon Mithridates' army, who had set themselves up in the town of Pelusium. Mithridates valiantly defended against the siege long enough for Caesar to arrive, and when he did the tides quickly turned. In almost no time at all the Egyptian forces were utterly overwhelmed, and any defensive integrity they possessed quickly crumbled. Panic and chaos ensued amongst the Egyptian ranks, and before long it was clear that the battle was lost.

As the Egyptian army fell apart, Ptolemy made his escape. He, with the help of a small band of soldiers, made it to a ship to flee down the Nile river. In their haste, Ptolemy's men neglected the weight regulations of their escape vessel, and their over packed ship sunk. Everyone onboard, including King Ptolemy, perished. Ptolemy, the ruler of Egypt's greatest city, now sat at the bottom of Egypt's greatest river, his lungs filled with water. The battle was over and Caesar could now claim yet another victory over foreign opposition. Back in Alexandria, what forces remained quickly laid down their arms and handed the city over to Caesar. He could now do what he had remained in Egypt to do in the first place. In mid-47 BC Cleopatra was instated as the ruler of the country, through the will of her father Ptolemy XII, and the decree of Caesar. Arsinoe, the only person of interest that survived the final battle, was banished and Cleopatra's rule was firmly secured. She, along with Caesar, now had the whole of Egypt in the palms of their hands.

. . .

We may often think of Caesar as a God, or as a mythological force of nature, but we can't forget that in actuality he was just a man. He was a man with desires and dreams, and a man who knew when he had pushed himself to his limit. Caesar now, more than anything, just wanted to take a break. He and Cleopatra had fallen into a heated romance while sharing close quarters in Alexandria for the better part of a year, and they longed for time to themselves and a chance to really enjoy their affair.

So Caesar took a break. Despite what threats still persisted throughout Roman territory, Caesar was ready for a vacation. He and Cleopatra spent the next few months sailing around Egypt. They travelled the whole country, enjoying each other's company and the relative peace that was now established across Egypt. It had been far too long since Caesar had been able to enjoy anything but victory over his enemies, and he was glad to put all of his focus on the beautiful Cleopatra, and take time off from concerning himself with the problems of the outside world.

The most ironic thing about this little getaway, though, is probably the fact that Caesar's civil war was technically still in operation. Pompey's defeat marked a significant blow to the Optimates, but that threat had not been totally stamped out yet. Optimate senators were raising hell in both Spain and Africa, and they began to pose a real threat to Caesar. It was clear that the fantasy he was living out with Cleopatra was nothing more than a fantasy, and he would have to return to reality soon. His enemies weren't going to wait for the honeymoon to end, and so Caesar had to prepare himself for the next stage in his civil war.

Chapter 8

The Final Sweep

Caesar's enemies, unsurprisingly, used Caesar's preoccupation with Egypt, and his subsequent absence from the political or military stage to their advantage. In multiple directions enemies of Caesar's authority were building their strength, and turbulence persisted outside of the Egyptian border.

When Caesar called an end to his non-involvement, he had a number of matters to attend to. The first order of business concerned Pharnaces II, king of Pontus. Pharnaces held allegiance to neither side of Caesar's civil war, but he used the war to his country's own advantage. Pharnaces was the son of King Mithridates VI, who had lost much of his land to the conquests of Pompey. With the Romans totally preoccupied with Caesar, Pharnaces saw an opportunity to take back his father's lost land.

Pharnaces had been a growing threat since the beginning of the civil war, and Caesar's preoccupation with Pompey, and then with Egypt, only allowed Pharnaces time to build even more loyal and more numerous legions. His luck continued when Caesar had to pull forces that could have threatened him to aid in the fight against the Egyptians. Pharnaces saw little opposition to his takeover, and his advancements were met with hardly any resistance. It was clear that a dwindling Roman opposition was by no means going to manage to hold against his offensive. A revolt in Crimea against Pharnaces had bought them a little bit of time to recuperate, but Caesar's assistance was imperative if they were to keep themselves from being wiped out completely.

Caesar began his march north in 47 BC to deal with Pharnaces. He passed through multiple countries whose allegiance used to be with Pompey, and on his way he collected substantial payments in apology for supporting his enemy. After a few stops Caesar's army was well equipped to fight another huge conflict. Of course, Caesar was willing to accept options other than bloody warfare. He had other matters to attend to and was open to peacefully solving the Pharnaces issue. Pharnaces had been the only Eastern ruler who remained technically neutral in the civil war, and tried to use this as reason for Caesar to grant him clemency. In actuality, he had only used this neutrality to go on a pillaging spree of Romans who lived on his stolen land, and Caesar knew this. Thusly, he would only offer peace on his terms.

Pharnaces was to surrender his army and give up control of Pontus, while also paying reparations for the damage he inflicted on Rome. Essentially, by conceding he would agree to be beholden to the Republic. Pharnaces was actually on the verge of accepting this, until he saw an opportunity. Back in Rome, tensions were high and revolt was a daily threat. Caesar had sent Mark Antony back to deal with the situation, but it was quickly falling apart. Pharnaces knew that he was not the only issue Caesar was currently dealing with, and thought that he could hold out long enough for Caesar to leave and go deal with Rome instead.

It was here that Pharnaces earned his spot on the long list of ill fated foes who underestimated Caesar. His delaying of peace negotiations had an opposite effect of what he had intended, and the impatient Caesar decided he was going to take care of the situation then and there. Caesar marched on the town of Zela, and set up camp on a battleground where, ironically, the Romans had been defeated twenty years earlier by Mithridates, Pharnaces' father.

Caesar set up and built his usual fortifications, displaying his awesome might to Pharnaces. Unexpectedly, Pharnaces, instead of fleeing the site, launched his own attack, and brutal close combat broke out. Pharnaces' haste and overconfidence was costly, as the Pontic army quickly lost control of its ranks and was overwhelmed by the Romans. It was another slaughter as Pharnaces gathered up a small band of cavalry and escaped the battle scene. What was left of his army were either killed or captured, and in only four hours the battle was over and Caesar claimed an overwhelming victory. It was this swiftly decisive win that compelled Caesar to send a message back to the Senate. It was a simple message that read, "Veni, Vidi, Vici," which can be translated to "I came, I saw, I conquered."

Pharnaces made his escape to the Bosporan Kingdom, and quickly tried to regroup. Caesar would never hear from him again though, as after only a few small victories with a newly amassed army from Scythia and Sarmatia, he was killed in battle. Caesar, meanwhile, looked to the next conflict. He appointed Mithridates of Pergamum as the new King of Pontus, and set back out for Rome, as the situation there was growing more pressing every day.

. . .

In Caesar's absence, the Roman capitol had slipped into disarray. Roman debts were surmounting, and there was great pressure for the elites to do something about this. With the ousting of most Optimate influence in the Senate, Caesar was elected to serve a one year dictatorship over Rome. He came to this position around the time he arrived in Alexandria, and was obviously preoccupied for the tenure of his dictatorship. Caesar's focus was not on the grievances of the Roman people, it was on his own conquest.

The population of Rome was suffering gravely in the country's sharp economic downturn, and violence was being threatened more and more each day. Caesar thought that Mark Antony could quell some of the stirring animosity between the people and the politicians, but the plebian class was in outrage, and wanted to be heard. Antony was unsuccessful in this mission, and his arrival only saw more violence erupting in the streets of Rome. After this debacle, in Caesar's eyes, Antony had fallen far from grace, and the relationship between the two would never be the same.

When Caesar finally arrived at the capitol, the debt crisis had reached a boiling point and he wasn't going anywhere until something was done about it. Caesar's dictatorship was quickly coming to an end, and his best shot at nipping this debt issue in the butt would only come from his capacity as dictator. Majorly indebted himself, Caesar couldn't just cancel all debts, for fear of what it would do to the Roman economy and his personal reputation. Instead, he borrowed ideas from his long dead political rival, Sulla. Vast amounts of property had been seized throughout Caesar's conquests, much of which belonged to prominent Roman figures like Pompey. This property could sell for a serious amount of money, and likely make a sizeable difference in Rome's debt counter. Unlike Sulla, though, Caesar only claimed and sold property from his dead enemies, rather than causing more unrest by confiscating property from opposition who might still be living in said property.

The value of the property was unbiased, with Caesar's allies and enemies alike paying the same price. Caesar didn't even cut Mark Antony slack, charging him the full price for ownership of one of Pompey's luxurious estates.

As Caesar's dictatorship was coming to an end, he needed to secure political power for the following year. He and Marcus Lepidus were elected consuls for the year 46 BC. This consulship would be defined by political reform in a bid to stabilize the Republic as much as possible. Caesar realized the growing empirical power of the Senate, and he sought to spread the power out more, and create a more rigorous checking and balancing system. The Senatorial body was increased to 900, so that there were more Senators to fill more roles, and alleviate the growing power of certain sects. He also initiated two new praetor positions, and nominated the men for the positions himself. These moves had the doubled effect of not only dividing power in a more appropriate way, but gave Caesar a chance to put more of his allies in positions of power, two of which were new allies at his side as praetors.

All of Caesar's legislation was important in stabilizing the Republic, but Caesar's ulterior motives were getting the most attention. Sure, Caesar had spread influence to a greater number of men, but all of his additions were backing him, and acted at his will. By securing power for a wider range of politicians, he was discreetly driving the combined force of their power to him. Rome's government was extensive, but at this point it was essentially puppeteered by one man.

. . .

In just a short time Caesar had secured his grip on Rome's capitol once again, and felt confident in leaving things to run themselves there. He still had enemies in the world, and those enemies weren't going to sit around and wait for him. Caesar's next target was Africa, where Metellus Scipio and Caesar's greatest living adversary, Marcus Porcius Cato, were building a great army along with King

Juba of Numidia. Just before he was about to depart, however, an unexpected situation arose.

Caesar was mortified at the news that his most faithful and heroic legion, the 10th, had launched a mutiny. The 10th legion had been by Caesar's side, fighting valiantly in his constant wars for over a decade now. They had marched all over Gaul with him, turned against their own country to follow him into civil war, defeated Pompey in Greece, and stuck out the campaign in Alexandria. In this time they had heard many promises of retirement, yet now they found themselves being ordered to sail off to Africa for yet another campaign. Enough was enough, they thought. The 10th wanted to see their piece of the pie for fighting this endless war, and were going to use force to get it.

The 10th launched a violent revolt, and marched on Rome. Caesar single handedly dealt with this mutiny not through force, but through words. He met the 10th outside of the city and addressed their grievances. He gave them a quick apology for not giving them the recognition they deserved for their service, but then his tone immediately changed. He scolded the soldiers for turning on him after these long years of faithfulness, belittling them and comparing them to lowly citizens. He stripped them of their pride even further when he dismissed them. He claimed they were now useless, as their devotion to Caesar he had known before was now clearly broken. He offered them lands for retirement, and was prepared to send them on their way.

The 10th had been ready for battle, though, and this turn of events was not only unexpected, but it shamed the soldiers. They had expected more emotion, more pleading, more something from Caesar, but instead he disbarred them without hesitation. Caesar's reverse psychology worked perfectly, and before long the 10th was asking his forgiveness, and requesting re-admittance to his ranks. The 10th rejoined Caesar unpunished, and through only the power of incredible oratory Caesar curbed a revolt that could have had horribly violent results. He could now get back to the matter at hand.

At the very end of 47 BC, Caesar set sail for his next campaign. This time he was heading for Africa to meet the Optimates, with plans to finally finish off the opposition which had kept this civil war raging for years. With the help of King Juba, Africa had become an Optimate stronghold. Publius Attius Varus was governor of Africa after he had secured his own victory against Caesar's army, led by the late Curio, years before. Caesar's former legate, Titus Labienus, was also stationed there along with Quintus Metelluls Scipio. Cato was a bit further, in Utica, commanding the garrison established there.

The combined forces of these three men, plus King Juba's Numidian army, was significantly larger than Caesar's seven legions, but they were still timid to launch a total assault. Instead, they did what Caesar's enemies so frequently did, and aimed their attacks at Caesar's supplies. The first few months of Caesar's African campaign were characterized by minor battles and small land advancements from either side.

Caesar was feeling the pressure on his supply lines, and it was imperative that the supplies kept coming, particularly because of Caesar's growing ranks. The Optimate forces were rightly afraid of Caesar. Huge groups at a time would convert to Caesar's army, abandoning the seemingly hopeless prospects of the Optimates to earn Caesar's known clemency that he bestowed on his fellow Romans. As the Optimate forces dwindled Caesar began to gain an upper hand in the small battles taking place, and the campaign started turning to his favor. He had an impassioned army, one that was wholly loyal to him and furious towards the Optimates, backing whatever move Caesar chose to make.

A small naval victory near the town of Ardumentum sent Varus packing, and he abandoned his troops for Hispania. Labieus and Scipio realized their armies were weak if separated, so they combined all of their forces in Thaspus, the venue for their next great showdown with Caesar. It didn't even matter that Caesar was outnumbered, he was not going to act like it. His armies came to the gates of Thaspus on April 6th, 46 BC and were met with an Optimate force ready for battle.

Scipio's army may have been numerous, but they were lacking the fire that had driven Caesar's army to where they currently stood. A thirst for battle was sending Caesar's forces into fury, and when Caesar unchained the mad dog, that dog bit. Caesar, by unrelenting force, gave Scipio no choice but to engage in battle, but at this point it was too late. Scipio wasn't ready for this kind of attack, and his ranks crumbled almost instantly. He had gotten himself stuck on the small strip of land that was Thaspus, and could do nothing to retreat his forces, or gain any kind of regrouping position on Caesar. King Juba and his army of 30,000 Numidians watched from afar, and he retreated his men without even participating in the fight. To any observer, Scipio's defeat was obvious.

Not only was this going to be a defeat, it would be a domination. Scipio was pursued in his retreat by Caesar's unstoppable army fueled by bloodlust. In the retreat, as many as ten thousand men were cut down in a merciless slaughter. This was more than just a fight for victory in this battle. This felt personal, and the slaughter decisively sent a message to the rest of the Optimates.

In Utica, Cato received this message loud and clear. Labienus and Scipio had both managed to escape from Thaspus, and they were on their way to Utica, seeking help from Cato. Caesar, of course, wasn't far behind, as he wasted no time in getting his army back into formation to march onward. When Cato received official news of the Optimate's defeat, he knew it was over. He knew there was no hope for any sort of counterattack to be mounted. Caesar wasn't going to be stopped, and his army wasn't going to turn back for anything, with their allegiance sworn to Caesar and no one else. Cato, pushed to the brink, took the only course of action he thought possible at this point. He fell on his own sword, reconciling that it would be better to be dead than live in a world conquered by Caesar.

It was an untimely and gruesome death for one of Rome's most loyal and stately Senators. He stabbed himself with his own sword in privacy after retiring to his chambers. The first cut failed to finish the job, though, and as Cato lay on the ground slowly bleeding out, his son came into the room to find the grisly site of his own father's organs spilling out onto the floor next to him. Doctors raced to Cato's side, but he refused them, obviously in total acceptance of his fate. His son and others had no choice but to watch in horror as Cato tore his stomach wound open and ripped out his own innards. Within moments he was dead.

This news came as a shock and a disappointment to Caesar. He had intended to pardon Cato once he reached Utica, and allow him to come back to Rome and live out the rest of his days peacefully. Cato would be remembered fondly by those who still supported the values of Roman Republicanism and the Optimates, but his death marked one of the final blows Caesar needed to deal to the opponents of his civil war. He commented on Cato's suicide saying, "Cato, I grudge you your death, as you would have grudged me the preservation of your life."

The following month, King Juba followed in Cato's footsteps in a slightly more unconventional way. Him and the previous Cato supporter, Marcus Petreius, fled from Thaspus, but were met with another of Caesar's legions. They knew they didn't stand a chance, and these would be their last moments on Earth. Rather than succumbing to a slaughter, the two longed for a more honorable death, and so they fought each other to the death, one on one, in a professional duel of sorts. Historical accounts vary, but the general assumption is that Petreius killed Juba, and then himself committed suicide.

After seeing that Utica was no longer a viable stronghold, Scipio and the remnants of his army continued to look for a place to regroup. On their way to the Iberian Peninsula, however, they regrettably ran into Publius Sittius, a Roman mercenary and general of Caesar's. A naval battle between the two ensued near Hippo Regius, and Scipio got to taste defeat one last time as his ships sunk into the sea. Refusing to be captured and brought to Caesar, who would have likely pardoned him as well, Scipio killed himself, and went to the bottom of the Mediterranean along with the rest of his army.

The last of the Optimate leaders, Labienus, had fled to Hispania to join up with Gnaeus Pompeius and Sextus Pompeius, the sons of Pompey. Caesar did not immediately make his pursuit, instead, opting to return to Rome first instead. There were pressing social and political issues to attend to, and Caesar also felt he was long overdue for a triumph. Upon his return, four lavish celebrations were held for each of his conquests, Gaul, Egypt, Pontus, and Africa, and they became the most expensive and over indulgent celebrations ever thrown in Rome. In these festive processions, Caesar's imprisoned enemies, like Vercingetorix of Gaul, were put on display. Cleopatra's sister, Arsinoe, was chained up and paraded around the city, but was released after this bout of humiliation. The expense of his triumphs were reckless, but all too fitting for the immense ego that was now such a part of Caesar.

The majority of Caesar's time spent in Rome, this go around at least, was on social and political reform. Provisions that helped cement Caesar's power were brought to the people, under the guise of being useful and balancing legislation that would help create a more stable relationship between the Roman capitol and its great many provinces. Caesar took total advantage of the political system, even pushing provisions through that would help to prevent others from achieving the kind of success he had known. His five year proconsulship of Gaul was what allowed him to procure such incredible victory there, but Caesar made sure no other proconsul could serve for such a length of time, and thus have the opportunity for this level of conquest. Caesar was well aware of his hypocrisy, and it was all a part of his plan.

Caesar wanted to lift the spirits of the Roman people back up, and rebuild a proud and noble nation out of the turmoil he himself had caused. He oversaw the completion of multiple new buildings, including a glorious new marble forum, and a new temple built to honor the Roman goddess Venus.

Of course, there were many provisions which really only sought to benefit Caesar. The most significant was his creation of the Julian Calendar, a calendar reform that was made to more accurately align with major seasonal events. In this reform Caesar pulled his most egotistical and longest lasting move of his career, and renamed the month of Quintillus to Julius. Today, we call this month July.

Caesar's reforms would continue to have sweeping influence over Rome, and only saw his power grow stronger and more absolute. He filled the Senate with those who supported him, surrounding himself with political tools he could use to push through whatever agenda he wanted. With unbeatable support in his governmental ranks, Caesar was elected dictator of Rome again. This time though, his dictatorship would be longer than eleven days, or even a year. Caesar was given a 10 year position as dictator, and it was a position that he would use to forever change the political landscape of Rome. Before he could get that underway, however, he had one last foe to deal with. At the tail end of 46 BC Caesar set sail for his final military campaign. He was off to Hispania to quell the resistance movements of Labienus and the sons of Pompey.

Chapter 9

Julius Caesar the Dictator

Led by Titus Labienus, Gnaeus Pompeius, and Sextus Pompeius, the forces of Hispania were rousing a significant ruckus, and a rebellion seemed likely. These three powerhouses, a former ally of Caesar's and two of Pompey's sons, would never accept Caesar's power and his grip on the world. They were determined to push back, and built an army of their own. Recruiting was not difficult, as disparity in Hispania and many of Rome's other provinces was turning people against their rule left and right. In a matter of months, while Caesar was restoring order and gaining power in Rome, Labienus and the Pompeius's gathered thirteen legions and six thousand cavalry forces. They expected to be a considerable match for Caesar, but what they didn't expect was his timing.

Before the close of 46 BC, Caesar and his smaller army of eight legions and eight thousand cavalry arrived in Hispania to the surprise of the enemy. Catching them off guard gave Caesar leverage early on in the campaign, and gave him room to secure a few crucial cities. The beginning of the Hispania campaign was marked by only miniscule advancements and a virtual stalemate between the two armies. The fighting, though scarce, was branded with a new kind of ferocity, however.

The Optimate fighters were well aware of their position in this war. They were the last remaining forces of a great army that had seen itself decimated all over the known world now, and Hispania is where they would be making their final stand. This mindset culminated on the plains of Munda, in the Hispania campaign's most decisive battle.

Three months into 45 BC, the forces of Pompeius and Caesar met and marched towards one another in preparation for heated battle. In the ensuing conflict The Battle of Munda would earn its place as one of Caesar's most intense battles ever fought. The troops of both sides knew what was at stake. Caesar's forces fought hard to crush the Optimates once and for all, yet Pompeius' forces fought equally hard to preserve a party that was on its last leg. The ethics of war were thrown out the window, with prisoners being mercilessly executed in either camp, and both sides fighting with malicious intent to destroy their enemies.

It was a tireless effort from both sides, with either gaining the advantage and disadvantage multiple times throughout the battle. Caesar himself admitted it to be a campaign with brutality unmatched to any before it. He would later recount the battle to friends and colleagues, saying that in all of his other battles, he had fought for victory. At Munda, however, he fought for his life.

For what likely seemed like eternity, the battle raged on with neither side holding any sort of upper hand. That was until Caesar's 10th legion, a legion which had previously revolted against the army, came to save the day. From the right wing, the 10th made their push on Pompey's forces. Forces from Pompey's right wing had to relocate and reinforce the left wing which was crumbling under the gallant onslaught of the 10th. Caesar immediately took advantage of the newly weakened flank, and charged his cavalry in with gusto. Labienus was in charge of Pompey's cavalry, and he broke them off from the main fighting to retreat to the camp which was lacking reinforcements. Upon seeing Labienus' retreat, Pompey's forces were struck with fear. They had just witnessed the one man in the army who personally knew Julius Caesar flee from the fray, spelling certain doom for any who remained on that battle field. What was an army descended into a chaotic mob of men fearing for their lives.

A retreat was attempted, but it was too late. Caesar was ready for pursuit, and he was going full measure with this battle. He would practice no mercy or clemency on the fields of Munda. As many as 30,000 men were butchered In Caesar's merciless rampage. Caesar and all of his men were determined to make sure this battle was the last one. Labienus was one of the 30,000 dead, but Gnaeus and Sextus Pompey found their way out of the carnage and fled, though not together. Within a matter of weeks Gnaeus was found, captured, and executed, but Sextus managed to escape to Sicily. Sextus would remain a relevant thorn in Rome's side, but would be the last of the Pompeius lineage to do battle with Caesar.

What transpired in the months following Caesar's pitiless victory was a series of mop up engagements to quickly and quietly end what little resistance might be left in Hispania. During the campaign, Caesar's nephew Octavian accompanied him, getting a front row seat to his almighty uncle's military command. The young Octavian wouldn't forget what he saw in those short months. By mid-45 BC Caesar had finished off his opposition, and his civil war could officially be declared over. What was started four years ago with the crossing of the Rubicon had finally come to an end. Any hostile remnants of the Republic's old rule was gone.

Caesar was now truly unopposed, with a whole world of conquest before him. He was the greatest victor the world had ever known, and now he had complete and total control of civilization's most powerful empire. It is almost to no surprise that this seemingly perfect situation would take the turn that it did.

.   .   .

In September of 45 BC Caesar crossed back into Italy, and was on his way back to Rome to claim his seat as dictator. Confident in what his nephew might be capable of as a ruler, Octavian was named Caesar's heir to the title in his will. The Caesares lineage had grown stronger than ever before, and Caesar wanted to make sure that things stayed that way after he was gone. Many expected him to name his illigitemate child which he bore with Cleopatra as his heir, seeing as he had recently put them in a gorgeous villa just outside of the Roman capitol. However, a legitimate bloodline was more important to Caesar. The decision was kept a secret for the time being, though, and Caesar's will was stored away.

By October, Caesar had returned to the capitol, coming home to an endless stream of honors. Rights and privileges were bestowed graciously and plentifully, and Caesar denied none of them. His public image as not just a man, but a symbol, was coming to light. The name and image of Caesar became synonymous with Rome and its might. Caesar's face began appearing everywhere in Roman society. Literally. He had his likeness imprinted on coins, which marked the first time in Roman history that a still living Roman appeared on currency. He also erected three statues of himself, so his stalwart and intimidating presence could be felt at some of Rome's most signatory spots. He placed one of the statues in the temple of Quirinus, with an inscription on it that translated to "To the Invincible God." Placing his statue in this temple sent a clear message of what Caesar thought of himself. Quirinus was a deified representation of King Romulus, the first king and founder of Rome. Caesar clearly thought himself worthy of having his likeness bask in the glow of Roman history's most important figure. These were conscious efforts on his part to compare himself to the Gods, and this statue was not his last.

Another statue was erected on the capitol building, right next to statues of the seven kings of Rome. Caesar was writing history in the present, placing himself alongside a rich part of Rome's history. Next to his own statue he erected a statue of Lucius Junius Brutus, the man who had commanded the revolt which overthrew the seven kings. It was an ingenious use of one of Rome's most dramatic political shifts to foreshadow Caesar's own intentions of pushing through another, even more dramatic shift.

The third statue of Caesar was made entirely of ivory, and was present at all religious events held in public, which was required by law. Public processions are where Caesar worked to establish his image. He wore lavish purple robes to events, and adorned his head with a crown of laurel leaves. He also began to wear red shoes, which were indicative of kings in the times of the ancients. Caesar was as far from frugal as he could be when it came to sustaining this image. His spending was excessive for all public events, plus the grandiose estate that was being built for him using tax dollars. Yet the Senate just stood by and watched.

Caesar had broken all Roman tradition, and was ushering in a new era of thinking for the Roman people. He had placed himself above the old conventions of society, and sought to change everything. He also placed himself above Roman politics, which infuriated a relatively powerless Senate. As soon as Caesar returned to Rome, he relinquished his title as consul, and handed it over to Quintus Fabius Maximus and Gaius Trebonius without any deliberation. He ignored the typical election process and put the two men in power himself.

A significant portion of the Senate was greatly angered by Caesar's actions, but he still had more than enough support to do what he wanted without consequence. Caesar was granted consulship for the next ten years, and was given ability to hold any public office of his choosing, whenever he wanted. He could even hold Plebian offices like Tribunes. He was granted the title of Liberator and given Roman imperium, making him virtually untouchable. He was safe from prosecution, and also retained supreme control of all of Rome's legions. His birthday was even made a national holiday. Caesar was enjoying fame amongst the Romans that no leader before him had even come close to. His ego ran rampant, but at no time was he given the idea that there was anyone who wanted to challenge his authority. He was the one true ruler of Rome, and had no plans of ever relinquishing that title.

Caesar didn't maintain his general popularity just through his own luxurious expenditures, of course. He wanted to see his country thrive as much as the common people did, and social reform was a major focus of his dictatorship. He wanted to relieve the economic pressures causing tensions amongst the Roman population, and set out to create legislature which could do so. He passed a law limiting travel outside of Rome, which helped maintain a consistent supply of able bodied farmers residing on Roman land. He also decreed that any member of the Roman elite who killed a plebian would have his fortune stripped and given to the family of his victim. Perhaps his most benevolent decree was when he cancelled a quarter of all public debt, an act which surely won him the support of any common Roman citizen who was not yet behind him.

Caesar also enacted a major architectural reformation while dictator. Rome had grown into a massive city, but the artistic integrity of the structures had been lost somewhere along the line. Caesar didn't want the greatest power in the Western world to be characterized by plain brick structures. Instead, marble would be the aesthetic of the city, and elaborate marketplaces and courthouses began their construction along with a new Rostra made entirely of the precious material. A public library also commenced its construction under the supervision of Caesar. He wanted to restore Rome to its former glory by giving it a whole new face and a whole new attitude, but this progressiveness was still met with anger in the Senate. The animosity persisted, but the aristocratic elites never voiced their concerns to

Caesar directly. Instead they plotted, and waited, and let Caesar go about his actions seemingly without a care.

The Senate's greatest fear was that Caesar was vying for the title of King. He had already been named Prater Patriae and Dictator Perpetuus, which translated to Father of the Country and Dictator for Life, respectively. Dictator Perpetuus even began showing up on the coinage which Caesar distributed. The next highest political position he could assume was king, and the senate worried this was the endgame in Caesar's plans. His godlike status was already taking shape, and he was on the verge of being worshipped. Many Senate members speculated that Julius Caesar was ready to become King Caesar.

However, Caesar never claimed this title for himself. In fact, he even refused it on multiple occasions. Taking kingship of Rome would have many ramifications that Caesar was not ready for. The Senate would obviously turn vehemently against him, and the already present rift would be ripped wide open. He wasn't even sure if the citizens of Rome could accept rule from another king, even though they had practically given the title to Caesar without saying it.

Being king for Caesar really was a matter of semantics. While he wouldn't accept the official title, he wasn't exactly going to disparage the comparisons. In all of his actions he permitted kingly parallels, and invited a royal image of himself through gaudy purple robes and the golden throne on which he sat during public events. One morning, the city of Rome awoke to find a crown placed atop the head of the statue of Caesar that resided outside the Rostra. Two tribunes removed the crown, and Caesar made no claims to be for or against their actions, or the actions of whoever placed that crown atop his head. There is speculation that Caesar might have staged this occurrence, as a way to test the waters for how people might react to a King Caesar.

Over time, Caesar's support of the idea of him as king began to show. When Caesar's supporters shouted out "King" to him from the crowd, the same two tribunes that had decrowned his statue had those citizens arrested. Caesar ordered their release, and then revoked the powers of the two tribunes. As time pressed on, Caesar showed less opposition to a title of King, and the Senate grew increasingly concerned.

. . .

February of 44 BC saw the festival of the Lupercalia taking place, as well as another test to see if the people were ready to be ruled by a king. Caesar sat upon his gilded throne watching the festival processions take place, adorned in all his royal garb, when Mark Antony entered the Rostra to speak with Caesar. He had brought a crown with him, and offered it to Caesar. The crowd was transfixed on Caesar and how he would react to this. Their disapproval could be heard, and Caesar was quick to deny the offer. The crowd was in full support of Caesar's stance, but Antony nevertheless made an attempt to place the crown atop Caesar's head. Caesar, as dramatically as he could, stood up and proclaimed that,

"Jupiter alone is king of the Romans." The crowd went wild at this proclamation, making their stance on rule by monarchy very definitive. Whether this occurrence was staged by Caesar or not, it sent the message to him loud and clear that he should continue to deny any sort of kingly title.

The title itself was a technicality to Caesar, anyways. He already had all the power a king could ever want, probably with more reverence and public support to go along with it. He wanted to turn his focus back on military campaigns, and had begun planning the next stage of his global conquest. He had his sights set on Dacia first, then on to Parthia. With success in these two campaigns, Caesar could return a substantial monetary fortune to Rome. He could also avenge his fallen ally, Crassus, who had found his defeat decades earlier in a disastrous campaign against the Parthians. Conquest of this magnitude was also Caesar's best tool to secure a kingship because if they weren't going to accept a king with that many victories in his name, they weren't going to accept a king at all. Caesar was planning to depart with his armies on their next campaign in March of 44 BC. However, a group of conspirators within the senate had other plans.

. . .

At the onset of 44 BC a plot was hatched to overthrow Caesar. Gaius Cassius Longinus, Praetor Peregrinus for that year, was the leader of a group of about sixty members of the Senate who had agreed to take part in the conspiracy. Cassius already had a history of conflict with Caesar, both inside and outside the halls of the forum. During the civil war, Cassius had aligned with the Optimates and had led an attack on Caesar's fleet. When Pompey was defeated, Cassius and his legions fled towards Pontus in the hopes of joining King Pharnaces. Caesar intercepted the fleet on the way though, and forced a surrender out of Cassius. Cassius was then given the title of legate alongside Caesar, and he fought by his side in the siege of Alexandria. Despite his pardon, Cassius maintained a staunch grudge against Caesar, and that animosity was culminating to this assassination plot.

Cassius had managed to garner significant support for his conspiracy, but he needed the support of one Senator in particular. Marcus Junius Brutus, a close friend of Caesar's was a necessary inclusion into the conspiratorial actions. This wouldn't be an easy persuasion, though. Brutus had fought alongside Caesar in Gaul and then, despite aligning with Pompey during the civil war, was pardoned by Caesar and allowed to rejoin the Senate. Caesar took a liking to Brutus, and supported him politically on many occasions. Brutus gained significant influence with Caesar's help, and now he was being asked to turn on his friend and literally stab him in the back.

It was a troubling positon to be put in, but the conspirators needed Brutus to legitimize their plot. Brutus' ancestor had led the revolt against Rome's last monarchist government, and it only seemed fitting that the younger Brutus should play a role in preventing a new era of monarchy from taking place. Cassius was confident that, with Brutus' support, their actions would be validated and accepted. It took heaps of persuasion, but Brutus eventually agreed to become a part of the conspiracy, seeing it as his duty if he were to uphold any honor in the changing tides of Rome's politics.

With Brutus' involvement, the conspirators had grounds to act. Caesar was scheduled to depart Rome on March 18th, and if he were to leave for Parthia, chances are the conspirators would never have another chance of getting close to him. A victory in Parthia was sure to cement his kingship, and action would have to be taken before this transpired. The conspirators set their date for March 15th, 44 BC. This was the day that Caesar was to meet with the Senate to have them approve his title of King outside of Italy. Prophecy stated that only a king would be capable of victory in Parthia, so this was a necessary honor for Caesar to collect before he made his departure. When March 15th, or the Ides of March as it is commonly known now, came the conspirators, primarily led now by Brutus, were ready.

. . .

When Caesar awoke on the morning of March 15th, he found his wife Calpurnia absolutely distraught. Nightmares the night before had warned her of a threat to Caesar, and she begged him not to meet with the Senate that day. The business that was supposed to take place with the Senate was obviously important, but Caesar adhered to his wife's impassioned requests. He sent Mark Antony to the Senate to tell them he would not be coming that day due to "inauspicious religious omens", and they were free to go home. When Antony delivered this news, worry erupted amongst the conspirators. They had no better opportunity than today, and this plot absolutely had to follow through.

Decimus Brutus, of no relation to the other conspiring Brutus, was sent to Caesar's home to urge him to come attend the Senate meeting. He persuaded Caesar to cast aside his wife's silly and un-confounded premonitions and come to the floor where a very important decision for Caesar was being made. Brutus assured Caesar that the vote would go his way, obviously, and he should come to the floor to claim his title as King of all Roman provinces. Despite Calpurnia's insistent pleas, Caesar was convinced that he was being paranoid and had nothing to worry about. He proceeded to accompany Brutus to the Curia of Pompey, where the Senate was waiting for him.

Caesar was presented with two more bad omens on his way to the Curia, but continued to ignore them, both inadvertently and purposefully. Days before, the soothsayer Spurinna had warned Caesar to "beware the Ides of March."

As Caesar made his way to the temple, Spurinna appeared once again and Caesar, sarcastically and narcissistically told her,

"The Ides have come."

Spurinna's retort was short yet grave.

"Aye Caesar, but not gone," were the words that Spurinna spoke to Caesar in her last warning to him.

Just before reaching the Curia, Caesar was even handed a scroll by a man named Artemidorus which detailed the Senate conspirator's plot. Caesar was handed something practically every time he walked more than twenty feet in the city, so he dismissed this scroll like the many others he was used to receiving.

Finally, Caesar reached Curia, his mind free of worry, and likely just focused on the days ahead which he hoped would see major victories. The processions commenced accordingly, with Caesar taking his spot at the head of the forum. The normal custom was to have Senators approach Caesar with their grievances or requests. Once he had taken his seat, the sixty conspirators surrounded Caesar. While a particularly large group to approach him at once, Caesar saw nothing out of the ordinary. Little did he know, the conspirator's anxious wait was almost over, and their plans were now getting underway.

The conspirators each brandished a concealed dagger, waiting for the signal to strike. Tillius Cimber requested that Caesar pardon his brother, who was currently in exile. When Caesar refused this, a stance everyone knew he would take, the conspirators moved in closer. The alarms went off in Caesar's mind as he stood before the sixty senators, all eyeing him with fire in their eyes. As soon as Caesar rose, Cimber threw Caesar's purple robe off of him, which was the signal that the conspirators had been awaiting.

Publius Servilius Casca had placed himself behind Caesar, and dealt the first blow. He revealed his weapon and stabbed Caesar's shoulder. Caesar, in an unconscious reaction, grabbed Casca and returned the favor by stabbing him with his pen. Of course, by this point, the rest of the conspirator daggers were out, and they descended on Caesar, stabbing him relentlessly until his death. In the bloody chaos Caesar watched as his old friend, Brutus, revealed his own involvement in the plot, and dealt one of many stabs to Caesar's body. Dismayed at this betrayal, Caesar's arguably final words were,

"Et tu Brute?" which translates to "You too Brutus?"

Caesar's flesh continued to be pierced by conspirator daggers, until he reconciled his fate and hid himself under his toga while the conspirators finished the job. Caesar, stabbed twenty three times, was dead. His body lay under a blood soaked statue of Pompey, and as he drew his last breath, Caesar's reign over Rome came to an end.

Chapter 10

The Aftermath of Assassination

All out panic ensued on the Senate floor upon the grisly murder of Julius Caesar. Many Senators fled, unsure if Caesar would be the only victim of these knife wielding men. Brutus quickly calmed the situation though. It didn't take long before a massive crowd was gathering outside of the Curia, and Brutus took it upon himself to address them. He assured them that this move, while harsh, was only meant to secure the dignity of the Roman Republic, and take the system back from Caesar's unchecked grasp. He promised that there would be no violent power grabs made by the assassins, and that their only hope was to strengthen the Republican ideals of the Senate. He also assured them that Caesar was their one and only target.

Making Caesar their only victim would prove to be a huge mistake by the conspirators. Mark Antony was set to see some sort of vengeance against these assassins, as he had been just outside the Curia as a barrage of daggers entered Caesar's body. Fearing for his life, he fled the scene, but upon hearing that the conspirators had no other targets in mind, Antony was set to put a plan into motion against the vile beings who had murdered one of his closest friends. Expecting to be named as Caesar's heir in his will, Antony awaited the inheritance coming his way, and planned to use this advantage to amass an opposition.

    Much to Antony's surprise, this was not the case when the will was read. Antony was only left with a share of Caesar's fortune, a sizeable portion to say the least, but not what Antony had expected. Instead, the virtually unknown Octavian, who wasn't even in Rome at the time, was named heir. Antony's plans would have to change now, but he wouldn't just sit idly by while Caesar's killers walked free.

The day after Caesar's assassination, the Senate met to discuss what the recourse in these tumultuous times would be. The system was coming undone at an alarming rate, and they needed to act fast before things unraveled into anarchy. Marcus Lepidus led a strong opposition to the self-named liberators, standing against allowing any kind of liberty to those who were involved in Caesar's assassination. The Senate, with the stability of the nation on the line, decided against him and his supporters. They pardoned the assassins for their crimes and allowed them to keep their Senatorial positions, on the condition that they uphold the legislation of Caesar, and continue to recognize the honors which had been bestowed to him in life.

The Senate also made the liberators provincial governors, seeing as the city, full of Caesar's supporters and admirers, was a dangerous place for them to remain. These governorships would get them away from this potential danger, and also gave them control of their respective provincial legions. In the agreement, Brutus was given governorship of Crete, and Cassius was allotted the provinces of Africa.

Out of everybody involved with this mess, no one came out with as little as Mark Antony. His heir apparent status was wiped from existence, he had lost the majority of what he believed he would be entitled to out of Caesar's inheritance, and he would now have to sit back and watch the men who assassinated his friend, colleague, and brother-in-arm, flee to safety, at the behest of his own country's Senate. Antony's career was not often defined by political cunning, but in the days following Caesar's assassination he would muster up all of his political sensibilities to turn the tides of the situation.

Antony's request to deliver the eulogy at Caesar's funeral was granted, and the Senate had allowed a grand public funeral for the fallen champion. Antony's eulogy began with your typical praises of Caesar's might and accomplishments, but then it took a turn. He began to speak out against the liberators, defaming them and inciting anger. He also rallied support for the late Caesar by making it known that Caesar would be leaving a portion of his inheritance to the people of Rome.

Antony then thrust Caesar's shredded and bloodstained robe into the air for the entire crowd to see. Fury overtook the crowd, who hadn't forgotten, yet were again reminded of the compassion Caesar had shown to them. They amassed into a mob, and made torches from the flames of Caesar's funeral pyre. The mob marched on the estates of Brutus and Cassius, burning them to the ground and causing the liberators to flee the country to their respective provinces in haste. Antony was now revered as the people's champion, and had successfully ousted the liberators with the help of angry citizens.

With the will of the people, and a little bit of brute strength, Antony secured political power for himself amongst the Roman elite. Playing on the people's emotions for Caesar, he had their full and undying support. Meanwhile Octavian, who was still studying far to the East in Apollonia, had other plans. He was merely eighteen years old when news of Caesar's death and his naming as the heir reached him. Octavian found himself with an important choice to make. Rome was heated with Antony riling up the mobs against the still powerful Senate whose allegiance likely still lie with the exiled liberators. If he were to return to claim his inheritance, he knew it would likely mean conflict. He had the option of either fleeing farther East to hide himself amongst the ranks of Caesar's former legions in Macedonia, or returning to the capitol where he could either refuse or accept the inheritance.

    Octavian had grown up watching the conquests of his distant uncle, and was well aware of the legacy that Caesar had left behind. Octavian knew he had an obligation to live up to the name which had been bestowed upon him, and decided his best recourse would be to return to Rome, and thus began his march. His route to Rome was riddled with Caesar's former and current legions, and so Octavian, with the posthumous honor of his uncle, gathered himself an army as he made his way to the Roman capitol.

In April of 44 BC Octavian and his legions came upon Rome's gates. Antony, running the entire political show by now, ignored the obvious threat posted outside his doors. He had ignored Octavian's entire march, unable to take this ignorant teenager seriously. Antony's sights were set far beyond the city walls. Decimus Brutus threatened his strength with his governance of Cisalpine Gaul. Antony, with hardly an acknowledgement of the much more immediate threat of Octavian, marched on Cisalpine Gaul. Meanwhile, Octavian used the time to continue to swell his army. He managed to recruit an army of nearly 10,000 able bodied soldiers, including two of Antony's legions who had defected during their march to Gaul.

As the months wore on, Antony's focus stayed on Gaul, and as Octavian's army grew, the Senate saw an opportunity in him. Octavian's fresh eyes seemed easy to manipulate, and seeing that the Senate wanted nothing more than to get Mark Antony out of the way, he bore the perfect name to display to the people. Octavian took the name Gaius Julius Caesar Octavian and at the end of 44 BC was given official command of Rome's armies.

Octavian's bloodline immediately gave him incredible popularity amongst the Roman population, and his conquests had their full support. It also had the full support of the Senate. The army he had amassed would easily wipe out Antony's forces in the East, and once that problem had been dealt with they could drop Octavian altogether. Julius Caesar may have been an unstoppable political foe, but his predecessor, they thought, would crumble. Early in 43 BC Octavian began his march North to catch up with Antony, not knowing that he was nothing more than a pawn in the Senate's elaborate political game.

Octavian was accompanied by the Roman consuls that year, Pansa and Hirtius. In their first engagements, Antony's forces would decimate the armies under the command of the two consuls, and both Pansa and Hiritus would lose their lives. The onset of this war was a bloody one, with the forces of Octavian, Antony, and Decimus Brutus engaging in fierce combat. Eventually, Antony had to flee the campaign and joined up with Lepidus in Hispania. Their combined strength would focus on Brutus and the rest of the liberators slowly gaining influence in the East.

Octavian, on the other hand, declined to pursue Antony, and instead turned back to Rome. The Senate's true intentions with Octavian were becoming more and more transparent, as Octavian's land requests for his veterans were being ignored, among other negligence. Within time, the Senate's plan was confirmed for Octavian, and he knew a show of force would be necessary to turn the tides on these gutsy Senators.

Lucky for Octavian, the Senate had little in the ways of a defense to put up against him upon his arrival to the capitol. The majority of their legions were either occupied with Antony and Lepidus, the Liberators, or had already switched sides to Octavian's army. Octavian, with ease, took charge, demanding to be named consul, and for the land and wealth entitled to his veterans to be distributed. Most importantly of all, however, was powerful legislation which stripped the liberators of their amnesty, removing their protection from prosecution. Within twenty four hours they were all tried and convicted *in absentia* for the murder of Julius Caesar.

Octavian hadn't even reached twenty years of age, and already he had become the first person in the history of Rome to obtain power almost entirely by means of military force, rather than the political process. The Republic's previous leaders had all utilized significant support in the Senate to acquire their strength, yet Octavian did so simply through the will of the people, and their unshakeable devotion to the Caesar name.

· · ·

Mark Antony and Lepidus were not Octavian's true enemies. His concern was with the liberators and their rising power in the east. He had no time or desire for a war with men who used to be close allies and even friends to the man whose name and legacy he was carrying forward. Rather than continue their conflict, the three men met near the town of Bolonia to discuss a truce. Over the next two days the three men drew up a detailed alliance between them and their mutual plans for securing Rome's power and stability. They divided Rome's lands equally between the three of them. Their alliance would thusly be known as the Second Triumvirate.

Unlike the First Triumvirate, this second iteration of the powerful political alliance was not kept secret. It was made incredibly public. So public, in fact, that it was passed into law in November of 43 BC, essentially establishing a three way dictatorship between Octavian, Antony, and Lepidus. By military prowess these three men had gained complete political control over Rome, and had a clear path to take whatever action they wanted.

Their focus, obviously, was on the men who assassinated Caesar. In order to secure the funds for this campaign, the triumvirate harkened back to the days of Sulla by issuing hundreds of proscriptions, stripping as many as three hundred Senators of their property and, for some, their lives. By the end of the year the proscriptions had done their job, and the resources were in place for 42 BC to be the year the triumvirate would wage war against the liberators, bringing justice for their heinous actions against Caesar.

Between the two of them, Antony and Octavian commanded twenty eight legions in total, and marched this enormous force towards Brutus, Cassius, and the rest of Caesar's convicted murderers. The liberator forces were prepared though, having had two years since the execution of their assassination to raise an army. The two armies met near Philippi to do battle. Antony fought bravely on the left wing, while Octavian had to retire to his tent on the right flank, having fallen gravely ill. Antony's forces overpowered Cassius's forces, compelling Cassius to take his own life rather than surrender to Antony. On the right, however, Octavian's absence from the fight was not boding well. Brutus won the advantage on that side of the fighting, and both armies were forced to regroup and retreat, preparing themselves for a second conflict.

The two armies spent three weeks recuperating from a fight that had hurt both sides considerably. After those three weeks, though, Brutus was the first to make a move. He launched an attack on Octavian and Antony, but this time both commanders marched into battle with their army. With renewed leadership, the Octavian offensive was much more resilient this time around, and they quickly managed to secure victory over Brutus and the rest of his army. Brutus followed suit with Cassisus, and committed suicide after the battle.

After this successful campaign, Antony continued his march East while Octavian returned to Rome to settle political matters. He was facing considerable scrutiny from the people of Rome, as the proscriptions of the Second Triumvirate had left behind a reckless economy. Lucius Antonius, brother of Mark Antony, led a movement against Octavian, denouncing his actions and building support amongst those who were angry with the laws Octavian had proscribed. Lucius managed to oust Octavian, but quickly found himself in over his head in Roman politics. He left to meet with his brother in the East, and use their combined forces to return to Rome. This was unacceptable for Octavian, who already had enough threats mounting against him, so he cut off Lucius in his march towards Gaul, and claimed victory through Lucius' surrender.

Antony had stayed virtually uninvolved in these affairs with his brother, dubbed the Perusine War, and this apathy was the catalyst for a rift between Octavian and himself. The enmity almost led to battle, but the forces of Antony and Octavian, who had served together in countless engagements under their current general and the great might of Julius Caesar, refused to fight one another. Octavian and Antony had no choice but to reconcile with each other. They came together to recognize their mutual interest in global conquest, and devised a plan to continue their spread. Lepidus, the third triumvirate who was busy ruling in Africa, was left out of their talks, confirming that he was no longer a necessary player in the triumvirate's strength.

. . .

With the situation smoothed over and Octavian and Antony's alliance firm once again, Octavian was able to turn his attention to Sextus Pompey, the last of the Pompeius lineage. After the battle of Thaspus in 46 BC, Gnaeus Pompey was executed, but his brother, Sextus, fled to Sicily. He spent the years that followed preparing to live up to his father's legacy. He was raising a great army, and intended to use its strength to threaten Rome. He had been a growing threat for years now, and Octavian could finally do something about it.

Their armies engaged one another for years, with neither side ever getting anywhere close to a decisive victory. Eventually Octavian, Antony, and Sextus met to discuss a peace treaty. In this meeting the Pact of Misenum was written, and the fighting stopped. It was Antony who pushed through the agreement most vehemently, as this fighting was only going to detract from the monumental campaign that was planned against the Parthian Empire. Octavian was not so eager for truce, though.

Sextus was one of his uncle's few remaining enemies, and he longed for a victory over him.

As soon as Antony went back West, Octavian resumed the fighting against Sextus. He turned to Marcus Vispanius Agrippa and Titus Statilius Taurus, colleagues of his from his military education days who were now admirable generals of their own, for help in the naval battles being waged in this campaign. Lepidus also sent reinforcements from Africa, showing his support of Octavian's continued fight. He clearly held the same sentiments as Octavian. This was a campaign for vengeance, and Mark Antony wasn't going to get in the way of it. Octavian, surrounded by allies, got his decisive victory in 36 BC when Agrippa decimated Sextus' fleet and Lepidus and Taurus marched into Sicily, causing Sextus to leave behind his most fortified stronghold. In Sicily, Lepidus brought in an overwhelming force and Sextus' army was quick to surrender. Octavian commanded that the surrender be ignored and justice be served to his enemies, but

Lepidus indulged the surrender. Octavian viewed this act as treasonous, and turned Lepidus' forces against him. Lepidus was exiled that year, and would play little to no part in Roman politics for the remainder of his life. The following year Sextus was captured in Miletus. Octavian, without hesitation, had him executed, and the Pompeius bloodline was no more.

.   .   .

These definitive actions in the campaign against Sextus Pompeius were the final nails in the coffin of the Second Triumvirate. The alliance was broken, but a relative peace had been agreed upon between Antony and Octavian. Octavian would focus on maintaining peace and stability in the Western provinces, while Antony would be allowed to continue his campaign in the East. It was Egypt specifically, a place all too familiar to him, where Antony would rest his head for the coming months.

Sometime in 41 BC Antony met with Cleopatra to discuss Egypt's involvement in the campaign against Parthia. The meeting between the two, however, ended up having little to do with Parthia, and instead Antony and Cleopatra fell deeply entrenched into a love affair. Cleopatra proved her incredible powers of charm and seduction once more, because Antony had suddenly lost all interest in the Parthia campaign, and was now fit to stand by Cleopatra's side.

Antony began to adopt Egyptian customs and a more Eastern way of life, and Octavian along with the rest of the Romans took notice. He began to reject his Roman heritage and threw his full support behind the Queen of Egypt. This support culminated in his damning Donations of Alexandria. In these donations a significant chunk of Rome's eastern territory was handed over to Cleopatra, and she was given the title Queen of Kings. The donations established Caesarion, the son that Cleopatra had borne with Caesar, as the son of Caesar, and given co-rulership of Egypt alongside his mother, along with the title King of Kings.

In 32 BC Antony solidified his pact with Egypt even further when he married Cleopatra, which was the final straw for Octavian. He implored the Senate to go to war with Egypt, building Cleopatra up as the greater threat than Antony. She was on a path to becoming the Queen of Rome should she and Antony get their way. Perhaps their most ardent offense, to the Senate at least, was Antony's claims to wanting to establish a new Senate based in Alexandria. This pushed the Senators over the edge. They listened to Octavian, and war was declared. Antony, unsurprisingly, maintained his position alongside Cleopatra, and his honors as a member of Roman society were revoked, and he was officially declared a traitor of the state. War was on the horizon once again as Octavian amassed all of Rome's legions to begin their march, and Antony put together a combined might of Roman and Egyptian legions to defend against the incoming storm.

The armies that stood behind Octavian and Antony were some of the largest that history had yet to see, and it was clear that this war was headed nowhere good. However, the matched strength of the two armies resulted in a stalemate. Octavian called upon all his military resources to gain the upper hand, and it was Agrippa, the naval commander who had aided in Octavian's previous victories, that brought the edge. His successful naval campaign against Antony managed to cut off his supplies.

As the pressure mounted on Antony and Cleopatra, they had no choice but to attempt an escape. The escape, while technically successful for the two lovers and allies, did not go so well for the majority of Antony's army. Antony's fleet crumbled against Agrippa's blockade, with his ship and a handful of others being the only ones to escape. Antony's army on land surrendered without hesitation to Octavian. He could now officially declare himself Rome's victor in both the West and East. The Caesar name was working wonders for the young idyllist. He marched through the Eastern provinces to end any more Eastern opposition to him, and by the time he made it back to Rome he had firmly established what his command over Rome's armies was capable of.

After dealing with matters back West, Octavian returned to finish the job with Antony. Antony had bought himself some time, and was confident that a counter-offensive could be mounted in Alexandria with right preparation. He was proven wrong in no time, though, as Octavian returned with unapologetic might, and made short work of Antony's last attempt at fighting off the might of Rome. As Antony watched his armies abandon their efforts en masse, he realized it was over. Everything he had worked for after Caesar's assassination was gone. He found no other option than to fall on his own sword. With Antony dead, Cleopatra had lost any hold on Rome's forces which she might have had. Knowing Octavian would likely show her little mercy, Cleopatra took her own life as well.

Octavian was officially unopposed. He cemented his power by claiming ownership of Egypt, and having Caesarion put to death, removing the possibility of a challenge to Octavian's position as heir. Octavian returned to Rome a hero of the people, and even was in the good graces of the Senate. His plan now was to take his reputation and the power he already had secured, and use it to elevate himself higher than any Roman politician before him, including his late uncle.

Octavian served indefinitely as consul, beginning in 31 BC. This position allowed him to push through his agendas which would benefit him in the future. He unified the legions of Rome into one massive army which answered first and foremost to him, rather than their recruiting commanders. Octavian was praised by the citizens for his reformations, and was tolerated by the Senate for seemingly upholding the ideals of the Republican system. Octavian employed the strategies of his uncle to test the waters of whether he could one day assume the role of King, refusing honors and maintaining the guise that he was a solid proponent of Republicanism.

In 27 BC Octavian launched a plan to appease the Senate. He declared that he would be stepping down from power, opting for total retirement from politics. As Octavian knew they would, the Senate refused this idea, as the vacancy that would be left in Octavian's wake would likely lead to more civil war. A constitutional settlement was enacted, splitting control of the republic equally between Octavian and the Senate. Octavian was bestowed with total military control, and was given the title of Imperator. He then changed his name to one baring more royalty and exaltation. In 27 BC Gaius Julius Caesar Octavian became Imperator Caesar Augustus, with Augustus meaning exalted one.

Imperator had originally been a title used for military commanders, yet Augustus would change its meaning to parallel that of an Emperor instead. The next few years saw his imperial power swell, and he virtually took control of nominating every major position in the Senate. His rule brought the Republic to its knees. Roman Republicanism was finally dead as Augustus ushered in the next era of Rome's history, the Roman Empire.

. . .

The death of Julius Caesar had implications that none of his assassins could have expected. His removal from power spiraled Rome into an entirely new era of their political system. The Roman Empire would uphold for the next 1400 years, developing an extensive history with stories that almost rival the impeccable nature of Julius Caesar's. The Empire's might would wax and wane in the ensuing years, falling into yet more civil wars, and continuing to spread their borders across Europe and Asia. In this time Rome didn't even remain the capitol, ironically. As the Empire became divided by their Eastern and Western powers, the capitol moved to

Constantinople. This majestic city would remain Rome's stronghold until its fall in 1453. Rome then went through a glorious Renaissance, which would carry it through the next few centuries as a great influencer of the world. In the 1800's Italy was unified and established as an official country, with Rome being established as the capitol. Today, Rome still stands as the capitol of Italy, and is one of the most sought after tourist locations in the world. And if it weren't for Julius Caesar, who's to say any of that would have occurred?

Chapter 11

Modern Caesar

In and around the time that he lived, it is hard to find a sole individual more influential than Julius Caesar. He truly shaped the world at that time, politically, socially, and even geographically. He is one of history's greatest characters who did so much in his less than sixty years of life that it's hard to believe he only lived one lifetime. There is quite possibly no figure in all of Roman history more recognizable than Caesar. With so many other important figures throughout history whose conquests or accomplishments may have even been grander than Caesar's, why do we continue to maintain the relevance of this man? The answer? Because history remembers those who enact change. The most influential individuals in the history of civilization were not people who followed the status quo. They were those who went against the grain, and pushed the limits of conventional society. Caesar's life hit all these marks.

Caesar's political tact can be studied today and remains exceptionally relevant to today's political climate. Obviously, the Roman Senate on its own played a major role in influencing the United State and many other country's modern Republic system of elected representatives and senators who, supposedly, represent the interests of people across the country. Caesar saw all the holes and all the weak points of this system, and he exploited them. His cunning tactics of subtly securing power can be seen all throughout the globe's corrupt political landscape. While Caesar might have gone about his strategies in a more dramatic and extravagant way, the root of the act is still present. Caesar, like many of today's most powerful politicians, knew how to play the game, and understood the extent to which he could bend the rules.

Perhaps the most stunning thing about Caesar's grip on politics comes from his death. His death, and its subsequent ripple effects completely reshaped Roman politics. By passing on a wealth of military and political sensibilities to Octavian, later Augustus, he secured his legacy of rule bending and manipulation. The events that followed the assassination brought the Roman Republic to an official end, and in many ways this political philosophy died along with Caesar, at least in Rome's case.

What is studied and toiled over possibly even more than Caesar's political intellect is his military strategy. You would be hard pressed to find a more successful military general within that part of history, as few men knew conquests as great as Caesar. The modicum of imperialism is a pursuit nations would continue to undergo for centuries after Caesar's own exploits all across Europe and Asia. World superpowers spent much of the medieval and pre-modern eras vying for more control over the world than their enemies, in a quest for ultimate control over civilization. The means to this end have been grisly and shocking all throughout history, and Caesar could be considered a saint compared to others in history who shared his ambitions.

It is incredible to think that military strategy from a time when wars were fought on horseback with swords and arrows would influence our modern era of rifles and vehicles, but they do. Caesar's trench warfare was unprecedented, and gave him an advantage in many battles. Similar fortifications to what he built on the plains of Pharsalus or at the gates of Dyrrachium characterized the fighting of World War I on many of the same lands. Even the way Caesar commanded his armies was unique, and the loyalty he was able to garner from his legions was unprecedented. He constantly beat the odds, and returned victorious from some of the most seemingly unwinnable battles. For as many times as Caesar's life was on the line, fighting valiantly against forces all over the continent that wanted to see his head on a pike, it is truly an accomplishment that he always walked away virtually unscathed. It is certainly ironic that for all the swords which were swung near Caesar, it was a band of old men with daggers that brought him his demise. It is yet another element that makes his story one of such intrigue and excitement.

It is the riveting and melodramatic narrative of the life of Julius Caesar which also helps to make him so remembered today. His legacy is filled with all the elements of engaging storytelling. It is littered with betrayals, revolts, love affairs, and a constantly heightened sense of epic scale melodrama. His is the kind of story that inspires legend. Centuries after Caesar's time on Earth, William Shakespeare immortalized at least a part of the long and complex story of Julius Caesar in his titular play. The play revolves around Caesar's death and the events which followed, with Caesar himself not actually being a main character of the story. Regardless, his influence is made apparent as audiences witness the Roman

Republic fall to shambles after his assassination takes place in one of the play's first scenes.

Caesar also wrote extensively on his conquests, and his writings give us the most complete look into his life. These texts have lived on and helped build his legend. The majority of his writings were written with an omniscient perspective, meaning there was no narrator. This gave him, as an author, ample room to give himself praises from the third person. This likely did a lot to help elevate his legendary status. Of course, many writers throughout Rome's history gave their accounts of Caesar's escapades as well, verifying his might and influence through third parties as well.

Julius Caesar is a figure that will not be forgotten as history continues to produce great leaders and innovators. Over two thousand years after his death his name can still find its way into casual conversation. He is a standard for military success and political ingenuity, whose impact is unshakeable. He possessed all of the traits which would be passed down to history's other powerful leaders, influencing the likes of Napolean, King Louis XIII, Henry IV, and many of history's other most recognizable names. He was Rome's most storied character. He was Gaius Julius Caesar.

Bibliography

McManus, B. F. (n.d.). Julius Caesar: Historical Background. Retrieved May 16, 2016, from http://www.vroma.org/~bmcmanus/caesar.html

Julius Caesar. (n.d.). Retrieved May 18, 2016, from http://www.biography.com/people/julius-caesar-9192504

Gaius Julius Caesar (100 - 44 BC). (n.d.). Retrieved May 18, 2016, from http://www.unrv.com/fall-republic/gaius-julius-caesar.php

Caesar, J., Kraner, F., Dittenberger, W., & Meusel, H. (1960). *Commentarii de bello Gallico*. Berlin: Weidmann.

P., & Parr, H. W. (1915). *Plutarch's life of Julius Caesar*. London: Macmillan.

Caesar, J., Edmondes, C., Ekins, N., Daniel, R., Hirtius, A., Place, J., . . . Edmondes, C. (1655). *The commentaries of C. Julius Caesar,: Of his warres in Gallia, and the civile warres betwixt him and Pompey,.* London,: Printed by R. Daniel, and are to be sold by Henry Tvvyford in Vine-Court Middle Temple, Nathaniel Ekins at the Gunne in St. Paul's Church-Yard, and Iohn Place at Furnivalls Inne Gate in Holburn.

Shakespeare, W. (1599). *Julius Caesar: William Shakespeare.*

Made in the USA
Middletown, DE
14 August 2021